Hot Fudge Monday

Tasty Ways to Teach Parts of Speech to Students
Who Have a Hard Time Swallowing
Anything to Do with Grammar

Randy Larson

Illustrated by Patricia Howard

Cottonwood Press, Inc.
Fort Collins, Colorado

Cottonwood Press
107 Cameron Drive
Fort Collins, CO 80525
1-800-864-4297
www.cottonwoodpress.com

ISBN 1-877673-17-X

Printed in the United States of America

To my wife, Judith Ann, and my son, Gabriel Wallace Larson,
who let me go off each day to write this book,
then put up with me afterwards.

Table of Contents

Using *Hot Fudge Monday*

Hot Fudge Monday proposes to bring humor and a fair amount of joy to the writing process, while at the same time teaching students the basics about parts of speech — no small trick. When teachers hand out pens and paper to students, the mood in the room often darkens. Polite students try not to grimace. Add a grammar book to the picture, and the situation becomes frightening as eyes glaze over and catatonia sets in.

It is my contention that with humor, all things are possible. That means that students can smile, write and learn grammar simultaneously.

It makes sense to study parts of speech in the context of the writing process. It makes sense to find joy in putting words on paper, and it makes sense to learn how to use words skillfully. *Hot Fudge Monday* was written to make sense. More important, it was written to make sense to young people, using words and terms they can understand, in a context they can understand.

Hot Fudge Monday joins the study of words to the process of writing those words into meaningful sentences. The book consists of eight chapters, each one dealing with one part of speech: *verb, noun, preposition, adjective, conjunction, pronoun, interjection, adverb*. Students learn about the various parts of speech through short writing activities that are interesting, humorous and a bit offbeat. The exercises are purposely quite different from those found in standard classroom texts.

Teachers who find themselves bumping along through *Warriner's Grammar* may want to dish out a few pages of *Hot Fudge Monday* to supplement and vary the daily routine. Others may wish to use *Hot Fudge Monday* activities as a springboard to longer, more creative writing assignments. The book can be used by itself to teach the basics or as a supplement for those who prefer to stick to more traditional texts. Either way, students are bound to benefit by studying *about* language as they *use* language.

Randy Larson

Verbs

RUN GO DO FALL SIT WRITE SEE

HAVE BUY GRAB

SLAM FLY CRY

What Are Verbs?

LAUGH BAKE BUILD MAKE CLEAN

Are you bored? Do you daydream through most of the daylight hours? If so, it is possible that you lack the proper number of verbs in your life. Tests have shown that without verbs, life becomes dull, drab, dreary and slow. You want *action*? Get your hands on a verb.

Verbs move things — planets, people, cars, bikes, Rollerblades, sentences of all kinds. In all of the following sentences, verbs provide the action, the movement:

Marvin *slammed* his finger in the door and *howled*, "Get me some ice!"
Lisa *snatched* her briefcase off the counter and *ran* for the subway.
Juan *whined* and *whimpered* until his mother said, "Okay. You *can go* to the party."

Verbs are everywhere. Take a ride and you will see them littering our highways:

STOP!
GO!
MERGE!
YIELD!

Go shopping. Look at the signs in store windows and above merchandise:

BUY now!
SAVE!
CHARGE it!
TEST DRIVE this beauty!

Pick up a newspaper or a comic book or a novel. The verbs are the words that make you *see* what is happening:

Juanita *gobbled* three mini-pizzas and a burger before she *fainted*.
Ching *grabbed* a pitcher of orange juice and *sloshed* it in Juanita's face.
Juanita *bolted* upright and *gasped* for air.
"You *could have murdered* me!" she *screamed*.

Verbs are a very important part of the English language. They are so important that every sentence *has* to have one. Without a verb, you don't have action — and you don't have a sentence, either.

Name _____

Five Hundred Horsepower

Verbs are to sentences what engines are to cars — they drive them, energize them and pull them along, sometimes at breakneck speed. But speed is not the greatest measure of a verb; it is the power a verb generates that really matters.

For example, a sentence like "She *went* into the office after school" has nowhere near the impact of "She *sneaked* into the office after school." The word *went* is a one-horsepower verb, while the verb *sneaked* generates a good five hundred horsepower. It pulls us into the sentence by our eyeballs. We can *see* the girl nervously managing the door, looking over her shoulder, sliding carefully yet quickly over the threshold into the office — all with one word: *sneaked*.

Read the sentences below and circle the verbs that energize each sentence. If more than one verb moves a particular sentence, circle both verbs.

1. Melanie weaseled her way into my heart, and later I cursed myself for letting her in.

2. As he kneaded the bread, he wished it was Harry's face there on the counter, in a convenient, doughy lump.

3. She pounded the desk with a frozen fish and demanded complete silence in the room.

4. Doug snapped the head off a match with his thumbnail and stuck the flame into a pile of dry grass.

5. Nobody peered into the crystal ball without Ursula's permission.

6. Lenny snickered as Angela tiptoed into the room.

7. Antonio hurled the chocolate éclair across the room, and it plopped into the fish tank.

8. Marcy spit out her words like watermelon seeds, one at a time, straight at the prosecuting attorney.

Now write five sentences of your own with verbs that energize them. Circle the verbs in each sentence.

_____

_____

_____

_____

Name _____

Verb Variety

Every activity has its own set of movements and behaviors. Verbs describe these movements and behaviors.

List at least ten verbs for each of the activities below. Use verbs that are specific, vivid and alive. For example, don't write the verb *walk*. It's too vague. Use *march*, *stomp*, *skip*, *limp* or some other verb that portrays the *exact* movement.

Example

Bake cookies: *dump, pour, mix, stir, roll, flatten, shape, grease, bake, watch, cool, remove, gobble*

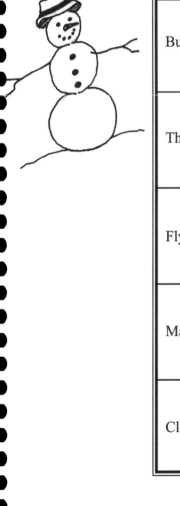

Build a snowman	
Throw a party	
Fly a kite	
Make a banana split	
Clean your room	

Verbs Alive

Good writing uses lively, active verbs. When sentences are dull, it is usually because the verbs are lifeless.

Rewrite each sentence below, replacing the dull, ordinary verbs in italics with verbs that are alive. Then add a sentence, using another verb that is alive.

> Ordinary: The wolf *came* to the door and *said*, "Let me in, or I'll *disturb* your house."
>
> Alive: The wolf *crept* to the door and *snarled*, "Let me in, or I'll *demolish* your house!" The three little pigs *huddled* in fear.

1. Philip *said*, "I love you, Elizabeth! Really!"

   _____

2. Louise glanced at the fruitcake and gasped, "Rashad, you've *made* a multi-fruited master-piece!"

   _____

3. Harold opened his jaws wide and *bit* off 12 square inches of pineapple pizza.

   _____

4. The beauty queen *walked* up to the judges and slammed her crown on the table.

   _____

5. Paula *took* off her mittens and threw them into the fire.

   _____

6. Walter *walked* into the bedroom and fell flat on his face.

   _____

7. The pigeon *sat* on the dead branch, mourning the loss of his friend Earl.

   _____

Pop Goes the Verb

You are a pop can. You have been popped, drained, smashed, bashed and trashed. Tell your story to your psychologist. You are on the couch. Life has been hard. Use vivid, interesting verbs to tell the tale of your miserable aluminum life.

(Decorate the can with the brand name and logo of your choice.)

_____

_____

_____

_____

_____

_____

_____

_____

_____

_____

_____

_____

_____

_____

_____

_____

_____

_____

_____

Name _____

Catastrophic Verbs

In the late summer of 1992, Hurricane Andrew struck the coast of Florida. The September 7, 1992, issue of *Newsweek* ran a lead story called, "Andrew's Wrath." The opening of that story contained these lines: "The storm splintered houses, flattened cars, toppled trees and whipped power lines around like children's jump ropes . . ."

Notice the verbs. They are powerful, accurate and moving: *splintered, flattened, toppled, whipped.*

Write a news report about a disaster that struck a city or village somewhere in the world, and use the most vivid verbs you can to describe the devastation. You could describe a hurricane, tornado, earthquake, flood, monsoon or volcano eruption. (You don't have to describe an actual disaster; use your imagination.) Use the space below for your first draft.

_____

_____

_____

_____

_____

_____

_____

_____

_____

_____

_____

_____

_____

_____

_____

_____

_____

Name _____

The *L*s Have It

Write a short news article using at least ten of the verbs listed in the box below. Circle each verb as you write. Base your news report on an event that happened in your town or in your school. (If your town or school is devoid of happenings, then make something up!) Use the space below for your first draft.

> lulled lynched lurched lounged loaded lapsed longed
> lolled logged loathed linked leered leaned loaned
> lapped lashed lanced lodged limped left leapt loped

_____

_____

_____

_____

_____

_____

_____

_____

_____

_____

_____

_____

_____

_____

_____

_____

_____

Name _____

Time Warp

Verbs do more than describe action. They also tell when that action took place — *now* (present tense), *before* (past tense), or *in the future* (future tense). For example, you can say, "Marsha brushed her poodle," if you mean that she brushed it last week, yesterday or even just a minute ago. If you say, "Marsha *is brushing* her poodle," you mean that she is brushing it right now. If you say, "Marsha *will brush* her poodle," you mean that she will do it later.

When writing, it is important to keep all the events in the same time frame. You don't want to start in the past tense, switch to the present, and then flip back to the past all in one paragraph. It won't make sense. The time warp will give readers a headache. Read the example below to see how confusing mixed-up tenses can be:

> *Abraham Lincoln, one of the finest leaders in American history, had a rough beginning. He hires out to other farmers to pay his father's debts. He lives in a lean-to along a riverbank, and he teaches himself to become a lawyer after going broke trying to be a businessman. Abe knew how to overcome hardship, because he will have plenty of it to overcome.*

The piece begins using the past tense verb *had*, then moves into the present tense *hires*, *lives* and *teaches*. The story then swings back to past tense with *knew* and then to future tense with *will have*. This kind of verb-switching will drive readers nuts.

It is very important to keep your verbs in the same time dimension. If your story happened ten minutes ago or ten years ago or ten centuries ago, use past tense and stick with it. If a story supposes what the future will be, then begin with future tense and stay there. If you want to tell something as if it is happening right now, start in present tense and stay in present tense.

Using your own paper, practice using the past tense. Describe something that you are trying to accomplish right now, but describe it as if it has already happened and you are looking back on the experience a year later. For example, suppose you are trying to learn to play the guitar. Imagine that it is a year from now and you have been successful. Describe what it was like to learn to play. What was hard? What was easy?

Be clear. Be concise. And don't forget to stay in the past tense as you tell your story.

Name _____

Tight Connections

Action verbs are not the only kind of verbs in the world. There are also *helping verbs*. Helping verbs are easy to overlook, just because they are so common. You see them everywhere. Here is a list of all of them:

is	be	am	are	was	were	been	has	have	
had	do	does	did	can	could	shall	should		
will	would	may	might	must	being				

Helping verbs appear along with action verbs, "helping" them tell time. For example, the word *is* indicates "now." The word *was* indicates "before." The word *will* indicates "the future." You wouldn't write, "I studying French when I visited Paris." You would insert the helping verb *was*, like this: "I *was studying* French when I visited Paris." The *was* helps show that you are talking about something in the past.

Sometimes some of the verbs in the box above appear alone, instead of "helping" an action verb. (Technically, they are then called "linking" verbs.) The linking verbs make connections, or links, between words in sentences. In the sentence, "The taco was tasty," the word *was* shows no action. But without the word *was*, the sentence would read, "The taco tasty," which makes no sense at all.

Rewrite the sentences below on the lines provided, using appropriate helping verbs from the gray box above. (You may use any of the helping verbs more than once, if you wish.)

1. "I been thinking, Billy."

   _____

2. What you thinking?"

   _____

3. "I thinking we ought to sell water balloons as a business."

   _____

4. "You kidding! We sell them with water, or without?"

   _____

5. "We sell them full of water, Billy. I not one to cheat my customers."

   _____

Name _____

Setting the Scene

Read the excerpt from *All the Years of Her Life*, by Canadian writer Morley Callaghan. Notice how many of the verbs convey a sense of weariness and sorrow.

> ### All the Years of Her Life
>
> Her face, as she *sat* there, was a frightened, broken face utterly unlike the grace of the woman who had been so assured a little while ago in the drugstore. When she *reached* out and *lifted* the kettle to pour hot water in her cup, her hand *trembled* and the water *splashed* on the stove. Leaning back in the chair, she *sighed* and *lifted* the cup to her lips, and her lips *were groping* loosely as if they would never reach the cup. She *swallowed* the hot tea eagerly, and then she *straightened* up in relief, though the hand holding the cup still *trembled*. She *looked* very old.

Write a piece of your own in which you convey discouragement to the reader through the actions of a person. Try to get the reader to feel what your character is feeling. Use any scene you wish. A couple of ideas: A girl could be sitting at her desk alone late at night working on a project that seems impossible. A boy could be sitting under a tree beside a pond thinking about how it used to be when his mom (or dad) lived at home with the rest of the family. Use the space below for your rough draft.

_____

_____

_____

_____

_____

_____

_____

_____

_____

_____

_____

Name _____

Rewriting Mother Goose

Choose any children's song or nursery rhyme and rewrite it into prose (story) form. A few suggestions: "Hickory, Dickory, Dock," "Humpty Dumpty," "Little Miss Muffet," "Baa, Baa, Black Sheep," "Mary, Mary, Quite Contrary," "Little Jack Horner," "Little Boy Blue," "Row, Row, Row Your Boat," "Three Blind Mice," "Pat-a-Cake," "Rock-a-Bye Baby," "Twinkle, Twinkle, Little Star" and "Simple Simon."

Use lively verbs, and circle each one that you use.

Example

There was a lady who lived in the country on a farm, and she loved it, except for one thing — mice. The place was loaded with them. They *raced* across the kitchen counters, *leaped* over the bread box, *dashed* under the refrigerator and basically *scared* her half to death.

The lady bought big yellow tomcats who *prowled* in the basement every night but caught nothing. She bought mousetraps that *snapped* down upon empty air. She *dusted* the corners of the kitchen with mouse poison but *killed* nothing.

One day the lady suddenly *snapped* under the pressure and *flew* around the kitchen, *slashing* at the mice with her carving knife. She *chopped* three tails from three blind mice who didn't see her coming. You never saw such a sight in your life.

_____

_____

_____

_____

_____

_____

_____

_____

_____

_____

_____

_____

Nouns

TOY FENCE BIRD ZOO GOAT CAT

SCHOOL STORE DOG

CAR BALLOON FORT

What Are Nouns?

ORANGE PENCIL PANTS MONEY

The first words you spoke were probably nouns:

Mommy!
Daddy!
Ball!
Cookie!
Remote control!

You learned nouns first because nouns are words that name things. You found that using nouns is much easier than pointing.

Remember pointing? You would see something you wanted, aim your little finger at it and grunt, and a whole posse of adults would race to get it for you. Then you discovered it was easier to say the name of the thing and watch the adults scramble.

Attaching a word to something gives it an identity, a name, but the process can be complicated. Pretend that you are 12 months old and you say, "*Ball*." The adults jump into action. Your mom, dad, grandma and grandpa all bring you a ball — a baseball, a football, a tennis ball and a beach ball. You start to cry because you wanted a ball with black pentagons on it. You should have said, "*Soccer ball*."

Nouns sometimes name things that you can "see," but not in the usual sense. These are things that have no physical shape — things like love, joy, peace, patience, intelligence, eagerness, alertness and boredom. Most people know what "joy" looks and feels like, even though they can't see it in the same way they can see a kitten or a lawn mower. Many nouns like "joy" name a quality or a feeling, rather than a physical object.

Along with verbs, nouns are probably the most important words in our language. Every sentence has to have at least one noun in it — otherwise you don't have a sentence.

Name _____

On a Clear Noun You Can See Forever

Here's a sentence that doesn't say much:

The man slipped on some food and hurt his leg.

We don't know this person. We can't *see* him. Is he a minister, a thief, a fireman, a fruit peddler? How was his leg hurt? Was it broken? Were bones sticking out? Where did this accident occur? When did it happen?

Here's a sentence that gets our attention:

Mr. Suave, our new history teacher, slipped on a blob of pudding in the lunchroom yesterday and cracked his shin.

We can see the guy now. We know who he is because the nouns have changed from *man*, *food* and *leg* to *Mr. Suave*, *teacher*, *blob*, *pudding*, *lunchroom*, *yesterday* and *shin*. These nouns make the picture clearer and more interesting. (If Mr. Suave had been your history teacher, and it had been your pudding he'd slipped on, you would probably be *very* interested.)

There are dead sentences just ahead. They are littered with vague, boring nouns. Rewrite the sentences, using nouns that readers can *see*. Be clear. Be specific. Use nouns that are alive!

Dead sentence:	A dog came to the school and made a scene.
Dead sentence:	A girl jumped into the water and saved another girl.
Dead sentence:	Two boys ate all the food.

_____

_____

_____

_____

_____

_____

_____

_____

Name _____

Common Nouns and Proper Nouns

There are two different kinds of nouns in our language — *common nouns* and *proper nouns*.

Common nouns are words that name things in a general sense: car, dog, person, building, state, music, book, etc.

Proper nouns name things specifically: Mercedes, Fido, Sandra Day O'Connor, Empire State Building, Delaware, "The Star Spangled Banner," *I Know Why the Caged Bird Sings*, etc. Notice that proper nouns are always capitalized.

When you use a proper noun you are getting very, very specific. And that's good. Readers feel more connected to you and your writing when they can picture things precisely. For example, you could write, "*I bought a car and a hamburger ten minutes after I won the lottery.*" The words *car* and *hamburger* are common nouns, nothing special. But if you wrote, "*I bought a Mercedes and a Big Mac ten minutes after I won the lottery,*" you would be giving your readers a specific picture.

Here's another way to look at it: Proper nouns stand out; common nouns blend in with the crowd. If you were in England on a summer day and Queen Elizabeth walked out into a crowd of 50,000 people, you would notice her instantly. You wouldn't pay much attention to all the common folk standing around.

The same thing happens when you use specific proper nouns in your writing. People pay attention.

Of course, you can carry proper nouns too far. You wouldn't want to write something like this:

> Mickey grabbed his Superfine Model 401 Fireblaster MicroTipped Hardroller Pen and drafted a letter to his grandmother Eunice Cornelia Hemmersmith III, then addressed and mailed the letter in a pale blue envelope made by the Gail Scowcroft Fine Letter and Stationery Company in Weak Willow, Washington.

You have to use good sense. It would be much better to say something simple like this:

> Mickey grabbed his favorite Bic and drafted a letter to Grandma Eunice.

Be sensible. Be descriptive. And be aware that using a proper noun now and then can give your writing a precision and exactness that readers will appreciate.

On your own paper, rewrite the sentences below. Replace the vague, general nouns with specific proper nouns.

1. At the arena, I cheered for the winning team.

2. Her car was far more expensive than our family van.

3. I visited a famous restaurant one day last week.

4. Meg got jeans, running shoes and a CD for her birthday.

Name _____

Replace Dead Nouns

Rewrite the sentences below by replacing the vague, lifeless nouns with common and proper nouns that are clear and specific. Use nouns that draw a picture in the reader's mind.

Example
Lifeless: The dog ate the man's shoes.
Alive: Toby, my toy poodle, ate Mr. Ribble's rubber thongs.

1. Someone climbed the fence and turned loose every dog in the pound.

   _____

   _____

2. The storekeeper's pet bird insulted the minister.

   _____

   _____

3. Our teacher accidentally rubbed chalk all over his face.

   _____

   _____

4. A chef in town uses leftovers to make snacks for his dog.

   _____

   _____

5. A boy hit a goat with his motorcycle.

   _____

   _____

6. My neighbor's car blew up last night.

   _____

   _____

Name _____

Muckberry Gazette

You are an editor for the *Muckberry Gazette*. A new reporter just sent in a story that is dull and needs to be rewritten by — guess who? (Don't whine. That's what editors are paid to do.)

Write in the specific names of people, places and objects. Use exact dates and times. Make the story clear and alive in the reader's mind.

Use common and proper nouns to your advantage, and remember to capitalize the proper nouns.

Train derails

A train derailed today on its way to a city near here, hurting some children and a few adults. Animals bound for a circus were injured when some cars collided with the end of the train. A spokesperson said that the accident was being cleaned up by some guys. People are asked to stay away from the wreckage until sometime tomorrow.

_____

_____

_____

_____

_____

_____

_____

_____

_____

_____

_____

_____

Name _____

More Muckberry

Below are *Muckberry Gazette* news stories that need some interesting nouns — desperately! Juice up these sorry tales with some specific nouns and proper names. Identify the people, places and things that make the story worth reading. Inject some life!

Eggs unearthed

Two men and one famous female archaeologist have found the eggs of a rare dinosaur believed to have roamed the dry regions of one of the western states many, many years ago. The scientists insist that a noted university should receive the eggs and begin testing for signs of life soon.

_____
_____
_____
_____
_____
_____
_____
_____

Shoplifters beware!

Two girls were seen entering a store in a town near here yesterday sometime in the afternoon. They left with some items that they didn't pay for, and the police are very interested in where these young ladies are at the present time. The store owner is upset and wishes to get her merchandise back and see justice done.

_____
_____
_____
_____
_____
_____
_____
_____

Nouns

Name _____

Be Sharp

You have witnessed a fire at the fireworks factory on Hauser Street. It was a horrible scene. You are writing a story about the incident for the *Muckberry Gazette*, a local newspaper.

Using sharp, precise nouns, write the first draft of your report below. Don't be crude. Don't try to shock the reader. Just give the facts in detail and let the reader see the events that took place, through your eyes. Circle all the nouns that you use.

_____

_____

_____

_____

_____

_____

_____

_____

_____

_____

_____

_____

_____

_____

_____

_____

_____

_____

_____

Name _____

What's the Dif?

Are you a student or a scholar? A teenybopper or a young adult? A know-it-all or an expert? An athlete or a jock? A reader or a bookworm?

Nouns make a difference. The noun you choose often depends upon the impression you want to make, or the image you want to create. Look at the difference a change in noun makes in the following sentences:

"*Officer*, how do I get to *Spider's Cafe*?"
("Hey, *cop*! How do I get to *Spider's*?")

There was a *person* on the front steps.
(There was a *corpse* on the front steps.)

It pays to choose nouns carefully.

Look at the pairs of nouns below. One noun in each pair is harsh-sounding, the other mild-sounding. Each is a perfectly good noun, but some nouns would be more appropriate in some circumstances than in others.

For each pair below, put an *H* on the line next to the noun that sounds sharp or harsh, and put an *M* on the line next to the noun that sounds milder.

1. _____ perspiration
   _____ sweat

2. _____ cabin
   _____ shack

3. _____ debris
   _____ trash

4. _____ news
   _____ gossip

5. _____ job
   _____ career

6. _____ guts
   _____ courage

7. _____ pimple
   _____ blemish

8. _____ alcohol
   _____ booze

9. _____ war
   _____ conflict

10. _____ underarm
    _____ armpit

11. _____ slammer
    _____ prison

12. _____ informer
    _____ snitch

13. _____ dirt
    _____ filth

14. _____ mess
    _____ trouble

15. _____ dump
    _____ landfill

Now come up with ten more harsh/mild noun pairs of your own.

Name _____

Leaving Home

You are living in Chicago after a breathless, exciting career in high school. You have an apartment that you are sharing with a friend, and you have a new job as a peanut butter taster.

However, problems have developed. Your teeth are rotting, the rent is going up and your roommate is making plans to marry a Brazilian trapeze artist. You want to go to the wedding, but you have no proper clothes and no money to get to Brazil. The landlord is getting crabby, and your boss wants you to work nights and weekends for the next 22 years.

What are you to do? You need to talk to someone about your problems. You need to get help.

You could phone home. Unfortunately, the phone has been disconnected, and you are out of money. You decide to write a letter to your parents, telling them about your difficulties and asking them for help. Don't make things sound *too* terrible, though, or they will make you come home and go to barber school — just as you promised to do if Chicago didn't work out.

Use mild-mannered nouns in your letter. Tell the truth, but tell it carefully. Write the first draft of your letter in the space below.

_____

_____

_____

_____

_____

_____

_____

_____

_____

_____

_____

_____

_____

_____

Prepositions

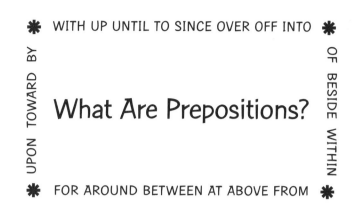

What Are Prepositions?

WITH UP UNTIL TO SINCE OVER OFF INTO

UPON TOWARD BY

OF BESIDE WITHIN

FOR AROUND BETWEEN AT ABOVE FROM

Prepositions in sentences are like wheels on a car — it's hard to make things run smoothly without them. Prepositions are often small words like *to*, *by*, *of*, *in*, *on*, *up*, *off* and *from*. They make up for their size by performing important tasks.

Prepositions show how one thing relates to something else. For example, suppose that you have a pencil, and you want to show its relationship to a desk. You might say it is *on* the desk or *in* the desk or *by* the desk or *under* the desk. *On*, *in*, *by* and *under* are prepositions showing how the pencil "relates" to the desk.

Sometimes prepositions relate one idea to another. For example, you might write to your mother, "I'm staying in Phoenix for the weekend," which means that you will be spending some time in Phoenix and not with your mom. But if you add "*in* the county jail," you have a completely different message — and a very aggravated mother. If you add "*for* armed robbery," your mother will probably become hysterical at the ideas these prepositions are relating. Mothers much prefer messages like, "I'm staying *in* Phoenix *for* an interview *about* a scholarship *to* Harvard."

Name _____

In the Beginning

Language probably began with one-word sentences. A cave man would rub his stomach and say, "Hungry!" The cave woman would hand the man a raw chunk of sabertoothed muskrat and say, "Cook!"

But when people started going to college, they needed several smaller words to fit in between the big ones, so that messages would be more exact. They invented words like *in, of, on, at, by, to, for, up, down, with, since* and *from*. They gave these little words a big name: *prepositions*. People started talking non-stop once prepositions were created, and there hasn't been a quiet moment since.

Rewrite the sentences below spoken by cave couple Og and Ug. Add prepositions as you see fit, from the box below. Circle each preposition. (You may also add words that are not prepositions.)

> within without with upon up unto until underneath under toward
> to through throughout since past over on off of near like amid
> into in from for during down by outside beyond between beside
> beneath below behind before at around among along against after
> across above about aboard inside

1. Og: "Sky dark." _____

2. Ug: "Rain." _____

3. Og: "Get wet." _____

4. Ug: "Hide cave." _____

5. Og: "No. Climb tree. Hide leaves." _____

6. Ug: "Afraid heights." _____

7. Og: "Before married, weren't afraid heights." _____

8. Ug: "Crawl hole." _____

9. Og: "Afraid dark." _____

   "You afraid everything." _____

10. Og: "I not afraid you." _____

Write at least six more lines, continuing the conversation between Og and Ug. Circle each preposition.

Name _____

Cleaning Up

Prepositions are small words with big responsibilities. Suppose that you say to your brother, "On our way to the store, will you drive me *by* the library?" You shouldn't be surprised if he drives on *past* the library on his way to the store. Brothers are like that. After all, you never said to stop. You said you wanted to go *by* the library. You should have said, "On your way to the store, will you drive me *to* the library?"

Practice being clear when you use prepositions. From the prepositions in the box below, choose those that best complete sentences 1–9. Write the prepositions on the lines provided. (Some prepositions will be used more than once.)

---

within without with upon up unto until underneath under toward to through throughout since past over on off of near like amid into in from for during down by outside beyond between beside beneath below behind before at around among along against after across above about aboard inside

---

1. The vacuum cleaner salesman knocked _____ the door _____ house number 2910 and braced himself _____ a smile.

2. Jill's father leaped _____ the dog to open the door.

3. _____ two seconds the salesman had reached _____ his pocket, grabbed a handful dirt, and tossed it _____ the living room carpet.

4. "I can clean that up _____ you," the young man said.

5. Jill's father looked down _____ the rug. He reached _____ the door and grabbed the broom. "Come right in," he said.

6. The salesman stepped _____ the threshold and _____ the pile _____ dirt he had just tossed _____ the carpet and started to untangle the hoses and gadgets he had _____ his hands.

7. "Now wait just one minute, young man," Jill's dad said. "You're going to clean this up before you leave, and I've got just the tool _____ the job."

8. "You mean you'll buy one _____ my fine, supersucking ZP 2000s?" the salesman asked.

9. "No. I mean you're going to buy my supersweeping B-R-O-O-M! Clean up this mess and get out _____ my house."

Name _____

Catching the Drift

Prepositions are words that work hard in everyday speech. They pop up everywhere and help "smooth out" our speech, the kind of speech you use with your friends, enemies, parents, teachers and coaches.

For example, you might say, "I went *into* the bathroom yesterday and found a pair *of* penguins *in* the tub." This is an ordinary statement that anybody might make after running into a pair of penguins in the bathroom. But listen to the sentence without the prepositions: "I went the bathroom yesterday and found a pair penguins the tub." Most people would get the drift of what you're saying, but what a clumsy way to talk!

Read the strange, preposition-less sentences below. Then rewrite them, inserting prepositions to help the sentences read more smoothly. (Choose from the prepositions listed in the box. You may use any preposition more than once.)

like	without	to	up	into	on	by	with	of	in	at

1. Nobody my family has a nose my dad's.

   _____

2. Whenever I'm Jennifer's house, I always start to sneeze.

   _____

3. Take the knife out that toaster, or you'll light up a Christmas tree!

   _____

4. Anyone any sense takes an extra pair shoes along when camping the mountains.

   _____

5. The time I reached Andrew, he was plastered artichoke dip.

   _____

6. I ran the stairs the bathroom, and slammed the door my foot.

   _____

7. Money, there is no reason to go shopping.

   _____

8. Always jog the morning; it's cooler, and no one sees you those strange outfits.

   _____

Name _____

The Correct Preposition, Please

Some prepositions can send you to jail. If the judge asks, "Did you drive *past* the store, or *into* it?" you had better hope that *past* is the preposition that applies to you.

Below are some questions that include some critically important prepositions. Answer each question as imaginatively as you can. Circle each preposition you use. Be careful. Jails are full of people who got caught by the wrong preposition!

The first item is done for you.

1. Did you disappear after the chase or before the chase?

   I was never anywhere (near) the chase because I was busy feeding the homeless.

2. Did you throw the diamonds beside the fire or into the fire?

   _____

3. Were you sneaking around the dorm or into the dorm?

   _____

4. Were you sliding up the pole or down the pole when Officer Blueprint yelled, "Halt!"?

   _____

5. Were you standing on his head, or were you standing on your own two feet?

   _____

6. Did you check the oven during the robbery or before the robbery?

   _____

7. Does the jury find for the defendant or against the defendant?

   _____

Name _____

Unnecessary Prepositions

Some people use prepositions when they shouldn't. It is a habit with them, like scratching their noses when they are nervous. They might say, "Where are my shoes *at*?" when they really should say, "Where are my shoes?" The word *at* is unnecessary and clutters the sentence.

Read the sentences below and rewrite them, eliminating unnecessary prepositions and any other words that clutter the meaning.

1. When do I have to return it by?

   _____

2. Where are we at in the story?

   _____

3. Why are you hanging around for?

   _____

4. Except for John, everyone but him is finished.

   _____

5. Where will you be sitting at when I come into the theater?

   _____

6. Where did you buy that interesting green blouse from?

   _____

7. I can't figure out where Jolene goes to every Tuesday afternoon.

   _____

8. You shouldn't have gotten us into all this trouble we're in.

   _____

9. Tell me where you put my radio at!

   _____

10. Where is your brother heading to?

   _____

Name _____

What Is a Prepositional Phrase?

Prepositions rarely work alone. They are almost always found with nouns (or pronouns), forming a group of words called a *prepositional phrase*. Prepositional phrases give additional information about nouns and verbs. They tell *how*, *when*, *where*, *what kind*, *under what conditions*, *how long*, *how much*, *which one* and *how many*.

Examples:

How: with a sneer, without a trace, like a shotgun

When: on Sunday, after this message, before sundown, during the trial, until I choke

Where: above his eyebrow, beyond the rainbow, inside the tornado, in Toledo, with me

Under what conditions: amid the confusion, under stress, for no good reason

Which one: with the yellow underwear, without a nose, beside me, under my toaster

Besides adding information, prepositional phrases can also add rhythm to your sentences. Ernest Hemingway's opening line in the novel *The Old Man and the Sea* reads: "He was an old man who fished alone in a skiff in the Gulf Stream, and he'd gone eighty-four days now without taking a fish." Notice the rhythm of that sentence — like the feeling of waves slapping against the bow of a boat. The movement within this sentence comes from artistic use of all the parts of speech, including the prepositional phrases *in a skiff*, *in the Gulf Stream*, *without taking a fish*.

It is important to know that even a long and detailed prepositional phrase is still a phrase, not a sentence. Many students will write something like this:

Before the entrance of the talented star of the extravaganza.

This is a series of prepositional phrases, not a sentence. Therefore, it needs to be finished before a period is used. Here is one way to finish it:

Before the entrance of the talented star of the extravaganza, the audience started getting restless and threw tomatoes.

Prepositions

Name _____

Prepositions in Concert

Prepositions always perform with a noun (or a pronoun). These preposition/noun (or preposition/pronoun) combinations are called *prepositional phrases*. Prepositional phrases can be short, like these: *to Mom, for John, at him*. Or they can be long, like this one: *for the curly-haired, blue-footed hipposaurus*. They always begin with a preposition and end with a noun, but there may be other words between the preposition and the noun.

The job of prepositional phrases is to add information to a sentence, and that information usually tells how, when or where something is happening, has happened or will happen. In the sentence, "The cow jumped over the moon," the phrase *over the moon* adds information because it tells where the cow jumped.

Circle the prepositional phrases in the first five sentences below.

1. We're not in Kansas anymore.

2. The power is in your slippers, Dorothy.

3. The monkeys dropped on him like a ton of bricks.

4. If you've got a water bucket and a smart scarecrow, you're in business.

5. Don't leave home without Toto.

Now write sentences containing some prepositional phrases of your own. Make your sentences about *The Wizard of Oz* or another movie you have seen recently. Put parentheses around the prepositional phrases.

6. _____

    _____

7. _____

    _____

8. _____

    _____

9. _____

    _____

10. _____

    _____

Name _____

Professional Phrases

Some prepositional phrases have had the honor of being used in famous books written by great writers. In the opening sentences from the novels listed below, put parentheses around the prepositional phrases. Then, on a separate sheet of paper, use any 10 of the prepositional phrases in sentences of your own.

A Farewell to Arms, by Ernest Hemingway

In the late summer of that year we lived in a house in a village that looked across the river and the plain to the mountains. In the bed of the river there were pebbles and boulders, dry and white in the sun, and the water was clear and swiftly moving and blue in the channels. Troops went by the house and down the road and the dust they raised powdered the leaves of the trees.

All Quiet on the Western Front, by Erich Maria Remarque

We are at rest five miles behind the front. Yesterday we were relieved, and now our bellies are full of beef and haricot beans. We are satisfied and at peace. Each man has another mess tin full for the evening; and, what is more, there is a double ration of sausage and bread. That puts a man in fine trim. We have not had such luck as this for a long time.

The Good Earth, by Pearl Buck

It was Wang Lung's marriage day. At first, opening his eyes in the blackness of the curtains about his bed, he could not think why the dawn seemed different from any other. The house was still except for the faint, gasping cough of his old father, whose room was opposite to his own across the middle room. Every morning the old man's cough was the first sound to be heard.

The Slave Dancer, by Paula Fox

In a hinged wooden box upon the top of which was carved a winged fish, my mother kept the tools of her trade. Sometimes I touched a sewing needle with my finger and reflected how such a small object, so nearly weightless, could keep our little family from the poorhouse and provide us with enough food to sustain life — although there were times when we were barely sustained.

Charlotte's Web, by E.B. White

"Where's Papa going with that ax?" said Fern to her mother as they were setting the table for breakfast.

"Out to the hoghouse," replied Mrs. Arable. "Some pigs were born last night."

"I don't see why he needs an ax," continued Fern, who was only eight.

"Well," said her mother, "one of the pigs is a runt. It's very small and weak, and it will never amount to anything. So your father has decided to do away with it."

Name _____

Make Your Own

The box on the left contains several prepositions, while the box on the right contains nouns and pronouns. Match any noun or pronoun with an appropriate preposition to create a prepositional phrase. Then put the prepositional phrase into a sentence of your own design. Write your sentences on the lines provided. Put some snap, zing, vim and vigor into your sentences.

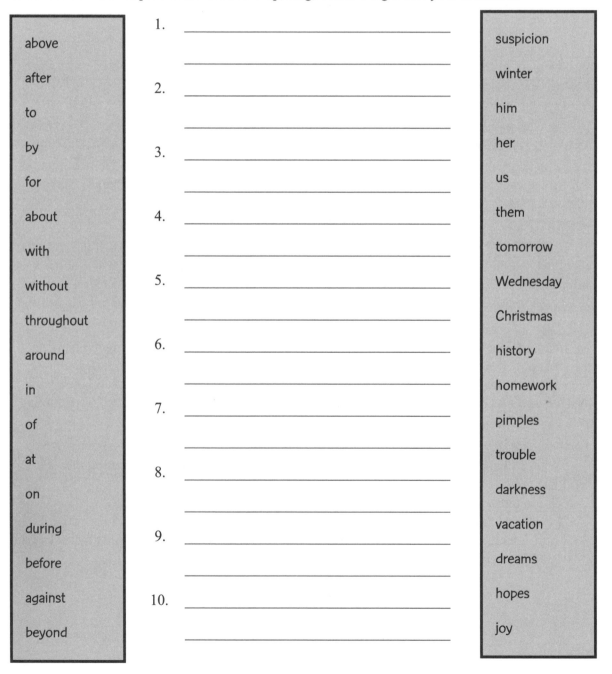

above		suspicion
after	1. _____	winter
to	_____	him
by	2. _____	her
for	_____	us
about	3. _____	them
with	_____	tomorrow
without	4. _____	Wednesday
throughout	_____	Christmas
around	5. _____	history
in	_____	homework
of	6. _____	pimples
at	_____	trouble
on	7. _____	darkness
during	_____	vacation
before	8. _____	dreams
against	9. _____	hopes
beyond	10. _____	joy

Name _____

Pick Your Preposition

Some prepositions are more important to some people than to others. One person might like the preposition *in* because he or she likes to be *in* on the secrets going around, or *in* on the punchline of knock-knock jokes, or *in* the right group at school or at work, or *in* the right neighborhood, or *in* line for Grandma's fortune.

Which preposition appeals to you? Decide on your favorite and write a paragraph or brief essay explaining why you like it best. You may choose any preposition from the list in the box. (Be sure to finish *in* time.)

within without with upon up unto until underneath under toward of to through throughout since past over on off near like amid into in from for except during down by outside beyond between beside beneath below behind before at around among along against after across above about aboard inside

_____

_____

_____

_____

_____

_____

_____

_____

_____

_____

_____

_____

_____

Name _____

Phrases From the Dark Side

Using at least ten of the prepositional phrases listed in the box below, plus at least five of your own, write a scene from your new vegetable horror novel, *Squash Cemetery*. See if you can write something horrible enough to keep your teacher awake for a week!

in the garden, on a sunny day, before midnight, after midnight, between the stairs and the doorway, under the covers, against the door, by the window, throughout the night, until morning, without a sound, amid the screams, of my little brother, past the cellar door, like the scream, of wet boots, in slimy muck, into the bedroom,
beyond the garden wall, beneath the ground, to no one else, with a deep sucking sound, like the screams of a coyote, behind the couch, in the shed, around 600 pounds, among the cabbages, along the fence, across town, inside my house

_____

_____

_____

_____

_____

_____

_____

_____

_____

_____

_____

_____

_____

_____

Adjectives

What Are Adjectives?

PRETTY SILLY GRUMPY HAPPY DOPEY

CUTE BRILLIANT

BLACK STURDY

BASHFUL COLORFUL IMMATURE SMALL

Adjectives are to a writer what paints are to a painter — they bring color, texture, depth and detail to the scene you are creating.

Suppose you were writing a short paragraph about a night when the moon was visible from your front lawn. You could write this:

One night I sat on the grass looking up at the sky. I saw the moon.

Or you could write this:

One *chilly fall* night, I sat on the grass looking up at the sky. The moon threw *cool, white* light down upon me as if I were in the spotlight on a *dark* stage and the crowd waiting in the shadows was about to explode into *wild* applause.

The words in italics above are adjectives. They add depth to the description and help the reader *feel* as well as see what it was like to be there on the grass looking up at the night sky. They give us more information about the nouns in the sentences.

And that is the main job of adjectives — to give us more information about nouns and pronouns. Because of their important job, adjectives are often the most interesting part of a sentence.

Name _____

Here's . . . the Adjective!

Adjectives are the spice of a sentence. They do a lot to make things interesting. Here is an ordinary sentence:

The sheriff held the pistol to the light.

The addition of one adjective adds some spice:

The sheriff held the *smoking* pistol to the light.

The adjective *smoking* changes the sentence by telling us something important about the pistol, and it suggests some interesting possibilities about what the sheriff is doing.

Adjectives are words that give us more information about nouns. They tell:

- the color of nouns
- the size of nouns
- the shape of nouns

- the texture of nouns
- the condition of nouns
- how many there are of a noun

Example

Three huge red ants crawled onto the glassy surface of the oval desk, ate most of a day-old enchilada and immediately got sick.

In the example above, the adjective *three* tells how many ants. The adjective *red* tells their color; the adjective *huge* tells their size; the adjective *sick* tells their condition. The adjective *oval* describes the shape of the desk; the adjective *glassy* describes its texture. *Day-old* tells the condition of the enchilada.

Circle the adjectives in the sentences below and draw an arrow to the nouns they describe. (Note: *a*, *an* and *the* are always adjectives. They are sometimes called *articles* or *article adjectives*.)

Example

Pouring (hot) (beef) gravy on (cold) pancakes is (no) way to start (the) day.

1. Sour music filtered out of the smelly basement.

2. A hot red dawn opened the sky in the east.

3. A pale white moon sat in the branches like a bird roosting for the night.

4. Nobody likes cold french fries with ice cream.

5. Black hate boiled out of his eyes as he looked at the crumpled car.

Jazzing It Up

Lifeless adjectives can make your writing dull. For example, look at this sentence:

It was a *nice* party. Everyone had a *great* time.

At first glance, *nice* and *great* seem like fine adjectives. But think about them for a minute. They give us nothing to see in our mind's eye. They mean nothing more than "better than lousy." The party would sound much more interesting if described like this:

The party started at midnight. Waldo brought his *golden* saxophone, and Myra brought her *new* drums, which she pounded all night until she broke the sticks. After that she used *Mom's silver* spoons from the *china* cupboard to play "Wipe Out!" We consumed *twelve giant* pizzas, *six dozen chocolate* donuts and enough *greasy* chips to fill a dump truck. By early morning, the house was trashed, and I knew it would take *ten* hours to clean up the mess. "*Fantastic* party!" Myra said as she stumbled past me, toting her *battered* drums. I didn't give a very *pleasant* reply.

It takes more effort to write a description like the one above, but it is worth it. Now we can *see* the party.

Rewrite the description in the box so that we can really see something. Use adjectives and nouns that will make your words come alive.

> Last night was the longest night of my life.

_____

_____

_____

_____

_____

_____

_____

_____

_____

Name _____

Brothers

Below are two columns of adjectives that are like brothers to each other. The adjectives on the left are mild-mannered ones, and their brother adjectives, on the right, are hot-tempered ones. Draw a line from the *mild* adjective on the left to the corresponding *hot* adjective on the right.

Example

MILD   HOT
ill-tempered   lazy
laid-back   vicious

MILD	HOT
1. upset	a. tight
2. particular	b. fat
3. overweight	c. skinny
4. unpleasant	d. cheap
5. decaying	e. gutless
6. inexpensive	f. hysterical
7. thrifty	g. bratty
8. slender	h. snooty
9. cultured	i. old
10. mature	j. filthy
11. soiled	k. fussy
12. timid	l. rotting

Sometimes mild adjectives are more appropriate than hot ones. Sometimes hot ones are more appropriate. For each pair of adjectives above, write one sentence using the mild adjective appropriately and one sentence using the hot adjective appropriately. (Make note of both the speaker and the audience for each sentence. Use your own paper.)

Examples

ill-tempered (MILD) and vicious (HOT)
- Teacher trying to be tactful to the parents of a bully:
  Edward can be rather *ill-tempered* at times.

- The President of the United States, explaining why he has sent troops to a battle overseas:
  Our troops will protect the innocent citizens from the *vicious* attacks of the enemy.

Name _____

A Deal You Can Refuse

Many people buy cars because they are influenced by adjectives like *sleek*, *new*, *powerful*, *sporty* and *inexpensive* in the advertisements they read and the commercials they see.

Suppose that someone has a car to sell, but she can't honestly use words like *sleek*, *powerful* and *sporty* to describe it, because the car is a real junker. She doesn't want to come right out and say so, so she tries this ad in the paper:

> Mature auto, 4-door, well-traveled, small. Traditional sound system, fog-lights, natural air conditioning, fully carpeted, needs some body work.

Remember, the car is a bomb. The seller has told the truth, but she has used kind, mild-sounding adjectives and adjective phrases to take the sting out of the truth. Draw a line matching the seller's words on the left with the real meanings, listed on the right.

1. mature

2. well-traveled

3. natural air conditioning

4. fully carpeted

5. traditional sound system

6. fog lights

7. small

8. needs some body work

a. A bowling ball fell through the floor last spring.

b. Two flashlights are welded to the bumper.

c. The scratchy AM radio is stuck on station KYUK.

d. The car is 48 years old.

e. The car has 241,689.9 miles on it.

f. The driver's window has a rock through it.

g. No one over 5' tall can sit in the car comfortably.

h. Sample squares from Wally's Carpet World are glued to the floor.

Now write your own ad for an obnoxious pet that you absolutely have to sell or give away, soon, before your father sells or gives *you* away! Remember — be honest, but make your adjectives kind and mild.

Name _____

Jailbird

You have a son who has gone astray. He held up a knitting store on Seventh Avenue, and now he is about to do five years in the penitentiary for his misdeed. You know, of course, that little Harold really didn't mean to hold up the knitting store. He has never done anything in his life that was his fault.

Using mild-mannered adjectives and nouns, write a letter to the judge of District Three, telling how sweet and innocent little Harold really is. Help the judge realize that Harold is a wonderful young man who doesn't deserve to be put in jail.

Some adjectives you might use: *rambunctious, immature, unpleasant, ill-tempered, unsure, timid, serious, caring, impulsive, cute,* etc.

Dear Judge Winkner:

_____

_____

_____

_____

_____

_____

_____

_____

_____

_____

_____

_____

_____

_____

_____

_____

_____

Name _____

I Love L.A.

Here is a letter you wrote to your best friend who moved to Los Angeles six months ago:

> Dear Twigs:
>
>   I hope you're having a great time in L.A. because I'm sure having one here. The other night I went out with some friends, and we went to a place and had some great food. The atmosphere was nice, and there was a singer who did comedy stuff in between the songs. Afterward we went out for a drive and had a super night. Wish you were here to have fun with us!
>
>   Bye!
>
> Love,
>
> Me

After you reread your letter, you realize that you haven't told Twigs anything. Which friends were you with? Who was the singer? What food did you eat? Where did you drive?

Rewrite the letter and add the details. Use interesting, exciting adjectives and nouns. Use the space below for your first draft.

_____

_____

_____

_____

_____

_____

_____

_____

_____

_____

_____

_____

Name _____

Snake Spit!

Below is a letter you wrote to your boss at Little Willy's Snake Shop in Big Draw, Texas. You want working conditions to improve, or you are leaving. You have written Willy the "nice" letter below, to try to help him understand.

Now rewrite the letter, saying what you would *really* like to say. You will need sharp, hard-hitting adjectives to explain your feelings (but keep the letter *G*-rated!).

Don't mail your version, of course, or you will be out of a job faster that you can say *snake spit*!

Dear Willy,
    I'm writing because I'm rather disturbed by something concerning my job. It would be better for business if you could possibly refrain from coming in at lunch and snapping your whip at the reptiles. They get excited, and it's kind of hard to feed them. They seem to want to approach me with their fangs out, and they curl themselves around my arms until I'm so numb that I can't reach into the bag for the Dinky Winky Snake Pellets. The snakes get hungrier and I get a little bit more nervous. Pretty soon the place is in a state of confusion. If you could kindly correct this difficulty, I would appreciate it. If not, I guess I'll have to find other employment.
Sincerely,
Your Employee

_____

_____

_____

_____

_____

_____

_____

_____

_____

Name _____

Ms. Silvershine

You are a counselor at Camp Runamuck, a summer camp for rich kids from England. One of your campers is a brat, and you want to write a letter home telling her parents what trouble this child is causing.

However, the girl's mother is Ms. Silvershine, one of the friendliest, sweetest camp supporters you have ever met. How can you write the letter so as not to hurt Ms. Silvershine's feelings? She must know the truth about her daughter, or the nastiness will continue and eventually drive you (and everyone else) nuts.

Use mild-mannered nouns and adjectives. Don't say, "Your kid is a jerk." Instead, explain what the child does that keeps her (and others) from having the best time of her young life.

This type of writing is usually not very much fun, but it is something we all need to practice. *Diplomacy* involves saying the truth in as gentle a way as possible. It comes in handy in life more often than you might expect.

Ms. Emma Silvershine
1212 Goldtone Drive
Big Bucks, England

Dear Ms. Silvershine,

_____

_____

_____

_____

_____

_____

_____

_____

_____

_____

_____

_____

Conjunctions

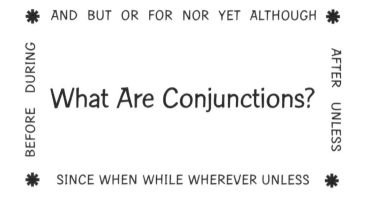

What Are Conjunctions?

When you look at a beautiful fountain with the water splashing over the cool stones, you don't say, "Look at the lovely mortar connecting those stones!" Nobody notices the mortar, not even the people who put it there. But everyone sees the pattern of the stones, with their unique shapes and colors made dark and vivid by the water.

So it is with conjunctions. They are the "mortar" between words; they bind other words, and even entire sentences, into one unit. For example, you might say, "I'm digging a hole and burying my poor dead cat." The reader concentrates on the actions of *digging* and *burying* and doesn't give a second thought to the word *and*. Yet without *and*, the sentence wouldn't look or sound right.

Another way to think of conjunctions: they connect things. Here are a few examples of commonly used conjunctions in our language:

> and but or for nor yet although because when
> while wherever since unless whenever

Name _____

Get Coordinated!

Some conjunctions have a fancy name — *coordinating conjunctions*. The name isn't as important as what these conjunctions do. They connect things that are roughly equal, like two sentences or two nouns or two verbs.

Examples
Alicia lies out in the sun all day *and* pays for it afterwards.
I'm not moving to Peru *or* Connecticut.
They said I would be eaten alive, *but* I swam on anyway.
I don't hate you, *nor* do I fear you.
I feel sorry for you, *for* you've never eaten a submarine sandwich.
You are all alone, *yet* you don't seem sad.

There are only six coordinating conjunctions:

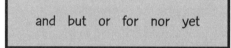

and   but   or   for   nor   yet

The most common coordinating conjunction in the English language is *and*. It is everywhere. Some words joined by the conjunction *and* are used so often, by so many people, that they're almost considered as one unit: *hamburger and fries*, *peanut butter and jelly*, *Bert and Ernie*.

On the lines below, write as many common *and* combinations as you can. You may include foods, places, teams, people, buildings, sayings, monuments — whatever works. Then get together with a classmate and brainstorm. Two heads are better than one.

See if you can complete a list of at least 20 *and* combinations. The first three are done for you.

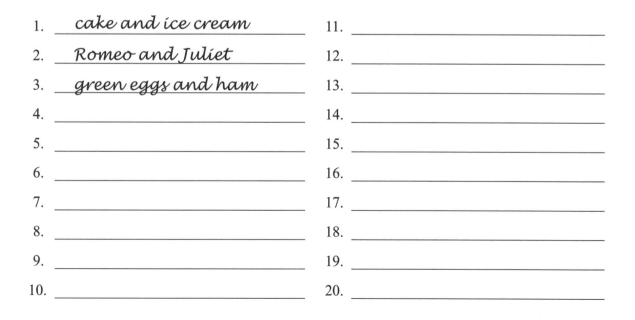

1. _cake and ice cream_
2. _Romeo and Juliet_
3. _green eggs and ham_
4. _____
5. _____
6. _____
7. _____
8. _____
9. _____
10. _____

11. _____
12. _____
13. _____
14. _____
15. _____
16. _____
17. _____
18. _____
19. _____
20. _____

Name _____

And You're Breathless

The conjunction *and* is probably the most useful of the coordinating conjunctions. However, too many *ands* can make any piece of writing appear ridiculous. Read the essay "Things I Hate to Wait For." After you catch your breath, rewrite the piece, eliminating some *ands* and combining ideas into sentences. Finally, add a few sentences of your own, including more "Things I Hate to Wait For."

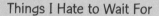

Things I Hate to Wait For

I hate the first second or two after I put money in a pop machine when I'm waiting for the pop to drop. And I hate waiting for french fries to thaw in the microwave and for the dentist to come back to the chair with the drill in his hand and for the VCR to rewind and for commercials to end and for the alarm clock to go off and for Saturday and for my luggage at the airport and for my name to be called in gym class and for the cat to come in from her stroll outside and for the light to turn green and for my hair to grow out after a bad haircut and for spring to come and for the six o'clock news to end and for copies on the photocopy machine and for Christmas and for a clerk in a department store to help me find socks.

_____

_____

_____

_____

_____

_____

_____

_____

_____

_____

_____

_____

Name _____

A Series of *Ands*

A list of items connected by *and* can get tiresome. It is usually better to turn such a list into a series. How? Just substitute a comma for each *and* except the last one. (Some people also put a comma before the remaining *and*, although many U.S. publications now leave it out.)

Example
    I fell and hurt my knee and my head and my back and my pride.

Revision
    I fell and hurt my knee, my head, my back and my pride.

In the sentences below, the word *and* is overused. Rewrite each sentence, replacing the unnecessary *ands* with commas.

1. Jed and Millie and Aaron and Hong and Shawna are all expert spies.

    _____

    _____

2. I don't want to go to summer camp because I'm allergic to grass and hot marshmallows and frogs and black-roasted wieners and team sports.

    _____

    _____

3. If you teach me how to develop photographs, I'll trade you my walkie-talkies and my two goldfish and my old stereo and my blue jacket and my little brother.

    _____

    _____

4. To write poetry, you must be sensitive and clever and wise and mysterious and brave.

    _____

    _____

    Complete each sentence below with a series of at least five items.

5. I love _____

6. I hate _____

7. Someday I hope I can _____

Name _____

Details, Details

There is an important punctuation detail to remember about the coordinating conjunctions *and*, *but*, *or*, *for*, *nor* and *yet*. When they are used to connect something big — namely, two sentences — you need to put a comma before the conjunction.

Let's concentrate on the conjunction *and* for now. If you use the word *and* to join a couple of nouns, you don't need any punctuation. (I'm going to the *mall* AND the *supermarket*.) Similarly, if you use the word to connect a couple of verbs, you don't need any punctuation. (I'm *borrowing* the car AND *going* to the mall.)

But if you join two complete sentences (also known as independent clauses) with the word *and*, then you need to add a comma before the *and*. Look at this example and revision:

Example
I'm going to the mall. You're not coming with me.

Revision
I'm going to the mall, *and* you're not coming with me.

Note: Sometimes, if two sentences connected by a coordinating conjunction are very short, you can leave out the comma, if you like.

Combine the sentences below, using the *comma/and* combination as necessary.

1. It's Wednesday afternoon. It's time to bathe the baboon.

   _____

2. Larry ran out of the room carrying the smoking VCR. Zeb got the fire extinguisher.

   _____

3. I want to be rich. I want to be gorgeous.

   _____

Put commas in the sentences below, only when necessary. Remember, a comma is needed only if the word *and* joins two complete sentences. If a sentence needs no comma, write "OK" beside it.

4. I'm going to buy an armored car *and* run for treasurer of Student Council.

5. I saved money for years to buy a trampoline *and* now that I have one I'm too depressed to bounce.

6. Elena and Jeff yelled *and* threw confetti at the winners *and* their coach.

Name _____

The Exclusive *Or*

The conjunction *or* is used to eliminate possibilities. Humans can be male *or* female, but not both at the same time.

The conjunction *or* has the same rule as the conjunction *and*: You need to put a comma before it only if it is used to join two complete sentences (also known as independent clauses). If it is used to join anything else, the comma is unnecessary.

Examples

Chill the pudding before serving, or you'll be wearing it. (The *or* joins two complete sentences, so a comma is needed.)

Please dive or jump or get out of the way. (No commas are needed because the *ors* join items in a series.)

Put commas in the sentences below, only if they are necessary. Remember, a comma is needed only if the word *or* joins two complete sentences. If a sentence needs no commas, write "OK" beside it.

1. Smile when you ask Ms. Keetz for a Kleenex *or* she will be furious.

2. Whether you climb up *or* down a mountain, you are going to shed some sweat.

3. You can have new shoes *or* a haircut.

4. Did you hear what I said *or* do you need to have your hearing checked?

5. To be *or* not to be, that is the question.

6. Do all of you have money *or* should we borrow some?

Imagine that you are babysitting 12 wild children from three different families, and you need to lay down some ground rules for survival before the evening begins. You might sit at the table and begin your list of rules like this: *You must put away all ropes and chains neatly in the closet, or I'll pull the plug on the TV.*

Finish the list with at least three more creative sentences of your own, each using the conjunction *or*.

Name _____

But Put in the Comma

The word *but* is a talented word. Sometimes it acts as a preposition, showing how something is an exception. (Everyone *but Pablo* had the flu.)

Sometimes it is used as a conjunction, joining two complete sentences. (I love you, *but* we have to break up.) When it is used to join two complete sentences, the conjunction *but* needs a comma before it.

Put commas in the sentences below, only if they are necessary. Remember, a comma is needed only if the word *but* joins two complete sentences (also known as independent clauses). If a sentence needs no commas, write "OK" beside it.

1. Keep your eyes open *but* close your mouth.

2. I suspect no one *but* you.

3. All *but* Jake were presented with a gold watch and a lobster.

4. I'm going to New Jersey *but* I'm going alone.

5. Louise ate everything *but* the creamed snails.

6. I told her about Eddie *but* she wouldn't believe me.

7. I will go to the play with you *but* first I have to floss.

8. Taming a cobra is a chore *but* it's not as dangerous as substitute teaching.

9. He seemed dead *but* we noticed his hands were still warm.

10. Everyone *but* Janet walked the plank with grace.

11. No one *but* a low-level louse would skip ceramics class to go snorkeling.

12. Evelyn called me a zucchini-face once *but* that was before I kissed her.

Using the conjunction *but* in at least three different sentences, write instructions for wearing the right clothes for the right occasion. For example, you might give this suggestion: *Be sure to dress in summer clothes for church picnics, but leave your bikini at home.*

Name _____

For the Love of Commas

Like the conjunction *but*, the word *for* is also talented. It can be used as a preposition. (I'm here *for* you.) Or it can be used as a conjunction. (I won't leave you, *for* our love is strong and pure and wise.) When it is used to join two complete sentences, the conjunction *for* needs a comma before it.

Put commas in the sentences below, only if they are necessary. Remember, a comma is needed only if the word *for* joins two complete sentences (also known as independent clauses). If a sentence needs no commas, write "OK" beside it.

1. I'm cancelling your debt *for* the good of our relationship.

2. I'm cancelling your debt *for* our friendship means more to me than a measly million dollars.

3. Mr. Howe, I'm sentencing you to five years of intensive babysitting at Little Munchkins Day Care Center *for* lying about the missing corn dogs.

4. Do you love me *for* my money or for my perfect teeth?

5. Janet took the leopard *for* a walk in Central Park.

6. Goldilocks flopped into the little bear's bed *for* she had travelled far and was exhausted.

7. Take your nose drops *for* it is sure to rain and turn cold.

8. The chef broke down and cried *for* he had lost his silver filling in the noodles.

9. All I want *for* Christmas is my two front teeth, a CD player and my own black-footed ferret.

10. Take care of your tonsils *for* they are your friends.

Using the conjunction *for* in at least three different sentences, write some sayings that would fit into *Dr. Wong's Wacky Book of Wisdom*. An example: *Never set a slice of pizza on your head, for you will end up wearing pepperoni earrings.*

Name _____

Yet and Nor — Say No More

The conjunctions *yet* and *nor* require the same punctuation as *and*, *but*, *or* and *for*. In other words, when they join two sentences, they need a comma.

Examples
I trusted you, *yet* you sold my collection out from under me.
I don't like potato chips, *nor* do I care for corn chips or salted peanuts.

Put commas in the sentences below, only if they are necessary. Remember, a comma is needed only if the word *yet* or the word *nor* joins two complete sentences (also known as independent clauses). If a sentence needs no commas, write "OK" beside it.

1. I don't like pigeons *nor* do I care to eat them.

2. Is Manny home *yet*?

3. Val has *yet* to receive any allowance for the first six years of her life.

4. I want to believe in Santa Claus *yet* here are all these uneaten cookies.

5. I don't believe in you and your ideas *nor* do I believe in this tonic.

6. I have *yet* to find anyone who got rich playing the accordion.

7. Jane hasn't called *nor* has she written in over ten years.

8. Omar knew his father wasn't coming *yet* he sat in the station and waited anyway.

9. Ms. Bolt is neither rich *nor* eccentric.

10. Have you cleaned your room *yet*?

11. I knew you liked rubber cement *yet* I didn't think you would eat it.

12. I have *yet* to meet a cheeseburger I didn't like.

Write three interesting sentences that need a comma and the conjunctions *yet* or *nor*. You might write advice to parents who want to know best how to raise their children. Or you might play the role of a pet psychiatrist and write advice to the owner of a neurotic dachshund.

Either/Or . . . Neither/Nor

Some conjunctions are married and should appear as couples in a sentence. When you want to say something that implies a consequence (something that will happen if something else happens first), then the *either/or* couple works well: *Either* you give me the keys, *or* I'm telling Mother.

When you want to make it clear that neither of two choices or situations will work, then the *neither/nor* combination works best: *Neither* you *nor* I know she really took the necklace.

Fill in the blanks in the sentences below with the correct conjunction combinations.

1. _____ you bring the poison, _____ I will.

2. _____ Carlos _____ Linda believed that Mark was dangerous.

3. _____ Felicia gets first prize, _____ I squeal about the videotape.

4. _____ Marvin marries me, _____ I'm selling his sled dogs.

5. _____ Monty _____ his mother could figure how the mouse got in the salad.

6. _____ John _____ I have enough money to buy our freedom.

7. "_____ pay me, _____ lose your breathing privileges," the man said.

8. _____ Santa _____ Rudolph could find Phoenix in the smog.

9. _____ you've got it, _____ you don't.

10. _____ your pizza _____ your fancy promises can keep me from leaving Tulsa.

11. _____ you brush between meals, _____ we don't kiss till Christmas.

12. _____ measles _____ the flu can take my mind off you.

Write a paragraph that includes two interesting *either/or* sentences and two *neither/nor* sentences about the Ding-A-Ling Brothers Circus, the worst circus in the world. You can take the role of a performer writing a letter of complaint, or you can be a reporter from the *Muckberry Gazette*, writing a review of the circus for the entertainment section of the paper.

Name _____

Use Them or Lose Them

Using the coordinating conjunctions *and*, *but*, *or*, *for*, *nor*, and *yet*, complete the sentences below. Write an appropriate coordinating conjunction in each space provided.

1. Sticks _____ stones will break your bones, _____ names can break your heart.

2. I heard your story, _____ I believe every word of it.

3. Plug the holes in that boat, _____ it will sink like a stone.

4. You must always tell the truth, _____ no one likes a liar.

5. You whine about the cold weather, _____ you won't move to Tucson with me.

6. You say you love me, _____ it's just a lot of talk.

7. If you've got cake _____ ice cream, you've got a party.

8. Life is a gas, _____ it can blow up in your face.

9. Surprisingly, neither Wilma _____ anyone in the band knew "The Star-Spangled Banner."

10. You'll have to leave by sundown, Big Bart, _____ you have worn out your welcome in Sludgeville.

11. Bring your ticket money, _____ you will end up on the outside looking in.

12. I'm not bringing my French horn, _____ am I helping clean up afterwards.

13. I'm glad I came, _____ otherwise I would not have met the beautiful Ms. Wimple.

14. I don't know whether to rent a billboard _____ send a singing telegram.

Write a sentence about a personal habit that you absolutely hate to see people demonstrate (eating with their mouths open, picking their noses, snapping their gum and blowing bubbles in your face, assigning boring homework, etc.). Be sure your sentence includes at least *one* coordinating conjunction that connects two complete sentences (independent clauses).

Name _____

Make Your Own

Use the nouns on the left in *conjunction* with the conjunctions in the box below to make sentences of your own. Use the conjunctions as often as you wish, but use each noun only once. (You need not use every noun in the box.) The first one is done for you.

and but for nor or yet

vandal
accordion
outlaw
truth
love
tickle
pumpkin
mothball
sea horse
rubbish
reindeer
punch
suds
plutonium
trombone
noodle
nectar
morsel
spinach
traffic
lightning
knuckle
keyboard
dumpster
inchworm
habit
gerbil
answer
ghost
concert
hostage
detective
crown
apple
flea
advice
bracelet
blubber
apricot
hamster
allowance
cocoa
vampire

1. *I found my accordion in the Dumpster, but I don't know who put it there.*

2. _____

_____

3. _____

_____

4. _____

_____

5. _____

_____

6. _____

_____

7. _____

_____

8. _____

_____

9. _____

_____

10. _____

_____

Conjunctions

Name _____

Write On

Use *all* six coordinating conjunctions (*and, but, or, for, nor* and *yet*) to write a news report about the appearance of a popular singing star at your school last Thursday at 1:00 P.M. The singer is a distant cousin of the principal, and the family is having a reunion at the park downtown on Saturday. The star has agreed to do a short performance at the school on Friday at 2:00 P.M., with the proceeds going to the school. Name the star, and name the songs. Be specific.

Circle each coordinating conjunction that you use. Remember to use all six of them.

_____

_____

_____

_____

_____

_____

_____

_____

_____

_____

_____

_____

_____

_____

_____

_____

_____

_____

_____

Name _____

Subordinating Conjunctions

As you learned earlier, some conjunctions connect things that are roughly equal. They are called *coordinating conjunctions*. Another kind of conjunction connects things that are *not* equal. These conjunctions are called *subordinating conjunctions*.

One part of a sentence is not equal to another part if it depends on the other part for its meaning. Look at this sentence, for example:

Pat loves to eat, although she is allergic to cooking.

Pat loves to eat makes perfectly good sense all by itself. It could stand alone as a complete thought. It could be independent.

Although she is allergic to cooking, however, *cannot* stand alone. It doesn't make sense all by itself. It depends on the other part of the sentence for some of its meaning. So — the conjunction *although* connects the dependent part of the sentence to the independent part and is called a *subordinating conjunction*.

Try this. Write the word *although* in front of one of the sentences below. Then combine the two into a single sentence.

Marvin loves Jamaica.
He is leaving the island.

You should have come up with one of these sentences:

Although Marvin loves Jamaica, he is leaving the island.
Although Marvin is leaving the island, he loves Jamaica.
Marvin is leaving Jamaica, *although* he loves the island.
Marvin loves Jamaica, *although* he is leaving the island.

In all of the sentences, *although* is a subordinating conjunction. Notice that it can be used at the beginning of the sentence or in the middle of it.

Using the subordinating conjunction *although*, try joining each of the sentences below. Don't forget to put a comma between the dependent and the independent part of each resulting sentence.

Cheri loves aardvarks.
She has never owned one. _____

Mikey eats mangoes.
He prefers enchiladas. _____

Evelyn loves winter.
She's afraid of the snow. _____

Name _____

Subordinating Combos

The box below contains a number of common subordinating conjunctions. Use them to help you combine each pair of sentences below into one sentence.

> after although because before if since though
> unless until when whenever where wherever while

1. I see an aquarium.
   I want to jump into it and blow bubbles against the glass.

   _____

2. Edwina keeps showing up at the circus.
   She hopes the Great Valentino will throw her a kiss from the high wire.

   _____

3. Dawn loves company.
   She prefers that the guests sleep in the yard.

   _____

4. Pat learned to cook last September.
   No one feels safe.

   _____

5. Gabe hates meatloaf.
   He stuffed his sandwich in Felicia's French horn.

   _____

6. Spot was a decent-looking dog.
   He got the measles.

   _____

7. You give me the keys to your car.
   I won't tell how you rigged the fog machine to belch.

   _____

Name _____

The Making of a Dependent Clause

Add a subordinating conjunction from the box to each of the sentences, forming a dependent clause. Then add words to complete a new sentence. The first item is completed for you.

> after although because before if since though
> unless until when whenever where wherever while

1. Amy buttered the toast.

   Although Amy buttered the toast, she wouldn't eat it. _____

2. Mavis lost her sandals.

   _____

3. Albert believes in himself.

   _____

4. People sneeze in crowded elevators.

   _____

5. Nobody believed Wilbur could have won.

   _____

6. Jody placed the custard pie in the box.

   _____

7. It became obvious that Mark was hallucinating.

   _____

8. Margot ate all the carbohydrates in the house.

   _____

Name _____

Subordinatium Gladiloli

Using at least five of the subordinating conjunctions in the box below, tell about your life as a potted plant. You sit all day on a small table in the lunch room at school. A cook brought you in last September to provide "atmosphere" at lunchtime. Since then, life has not been easy. In writing your heart-wrenching story, you might consider the following:

Is it better to be tall, green and beautiful than short, dry and stubby? Is there one special person who drops by every day and whispers something nice in your leaves? When people bury gum wrappers in your roots, how do you feel? Are there days when it is too quiet? How does it feel to be thirsty, and then have someone pour old milk on your petals? What would you say if you could speak the language of humans?

Circle each subordinating conjunction that you use, and be sure to put a comma between the dependent and independent clauses in your sentences.

| after although because before if since though during |
| unless until when whenever where wherever while so |

_____

_____

_____

_____

_____

_____

_____

_____

_____

_____

_____

_____

_____

Pronouns

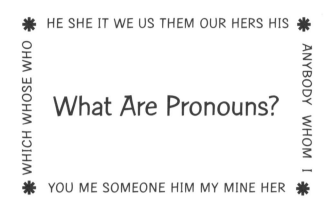

What Are Pronouns?

Actors and actresses who are about to take a hard fall usually stop and yell, "Stand in!" This means that someone else who resembles the star is going to have to tumble into a waterfall, jump from a burning potato chip truck, or leap out of an exploding helicopter.

Pronouns do the same for nouns. When a noun is about to wear itself out in a sentence, a pronoun can hop in. The sentence reads better, the noun takes a break, and the reader is happier.

Here is a paragraph that could use some more pronouns:

Meg stepped to the end of the diving board and looked down. Meg then turned back and looked longingly at her sister, who was perched safely on the ladder, smiling. Meg knew this was it. One! Two! Three! Meg ran to the end of the board, leaped, tucked and made one and one half turns, then straightened out like an arrow and hit the water cleanly. Meg knew Meg had made the best dive of her life.

Here is the same paragraph, with pronouns standing in for some of the nouns:

Meg stepped to the end of the diving board and looked down. *She* then turned back and looked longingly at her sister, who was perched safely on the ladder, smiling. Meg knew this was it. One! Two! Three! *She* ran to the end of the board, leaped, tucked, and made one and one half turns, then straightened out like an arrow and hit the water cleanly. *She* knew *she* had made the best dive of her life.

Here are some common pronouns:

> I you he she her him me
> them it yours hers his theirs
> mine myself yourself himself
> herself who whom whose which
> what anybody someone everyone

Name _____

The Case of the Pronoun Prank

The paragraph below sounds pretty strange. It needs some pronouns to stand in for the nouns once in a while. Rewrite the paragraph using pronouns from the box on the left. You may use the pronouns more than once.

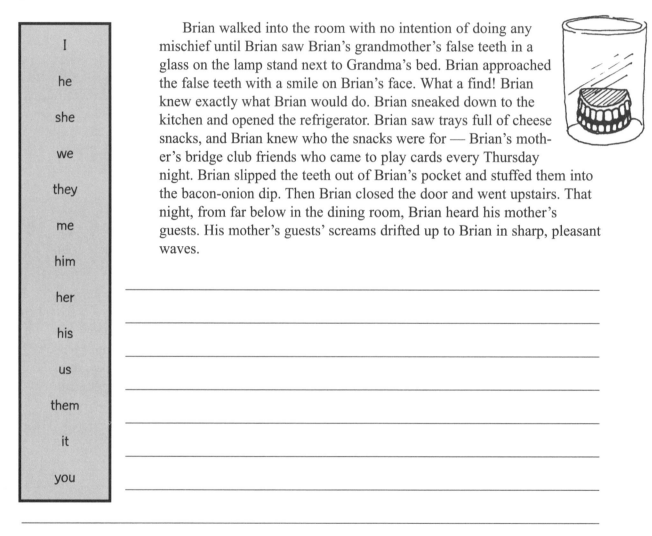

I
he
she
we
they
me
him
her
his
us
them
it
you

Brian walked into the room with no intention of doing any mischief until Brian saw Brian's grandmother's false teeth in a glass on the lamp stand next to Grandma's bed. Brian approached the false teeth with a smile on Brian's face. What a find! Brian knew exactly what Brian would do. Brian sneaked down to the kitchen and opened the refrigerator. Brian saw trays full of cheese snacks, and Brian knew who the snacks were for — Brian's mother's bridge club friends who came to play cards every Thursday night. Brian slipped the teeth out of Brian's pocket and stuffed them into the bacon-onion dip. Then Brian closed the door and went upstairs. That night, from far below in the dining room, Brian heard his mother's guests. His mother's guests' screams drifted up to Brian in sharp, pleasant waves.

_____

_____

_____

_____

_____

_____

_____

_____

_____

_____

_____

Name _____

Getting Personal

A *personal* pronoun is a pronoun that stands in for a *person*. (There is one exception. The personal pronoun *it* stands in for an object instead of a person.)

There aren't very many personal pronouns. Here are all of them:

> I he she we they me him her us them you it

As you can see, some of them are singular (*I, he, she, me, it*) while others are plural (*us, we, them, they*).

Read the sentences below. Then rewrite them, using personal pronouns from the list above.

1. When I turned on the lie detector, the lie detector told me the lie detector had a headache. Honest!

   _____

2. If the doctor ever shows up, ask the doctor if the doctor will deliver the baby.

   _____

3. "I can't believe you ate 39 kumquats," said Tom to Tom's brother.

   _____

4. Gertrude threw the banana cream pie at the judge, but Gertrude later apologized.

   _____

5. Alvin asked Tim to loan Alvin Tim's skateboard, but Tim said, "Buy your own!"

   _____

You are the captain of the Roughriders Ring Toss Team from Loose Tooth, Alaska, and your team is up against a tough bunch of competitors from Tennessee who have won six Ring-Toss Super Bowls in the past ten years. Everyone in the locker room, including NBC television, is awaiting your inspirational speech before the contest. What do you tell your teammates who have never gone this far before in post-season play and who are all used to playing outside with their mittens on? Write down the main points of your speech. Then circle the personal pronouns.

Name _____

"Self" Pronouns

The "self" pronouns are easy to recognize because they all end in "self." Here are all of them:

> myself oneself himself herself itself
> yourself yourselves ourselves themselves

Notice that some of the pronouns are singular (*myself, oneself, himself, herself, itself, yourself*) and some are plural (*ourselves, yourselves, themselves*). Notice that you don't see *theirselves*. That's because it is considered substandard English.

For each of the items below, choose the pronoun from the above list that best completes the sentence.

1. The twelve members of the Beagle family considered _____ the best bagel bakers on Beezle Street, bar none.

2. We were quite concerned when Stuart confessed that he believed _____ to be an artichoke.

3. Miss Apple always says to the class, "Behave _____ out there!"

4. Annette saw _____ as the only cop on the beat worth her uniform.

5. Beatrice considers _____ the roller blade champion of Junction City.

6. If you worry about the world too much you will tie _____ in knots.

7. "I declare _____ to be the winner!" Juan said, even before the starting gun was fired.

8. The tornado blew _____ out before it reached Kansas.

9. One must take _____ seriously in this class.

10. We humans see _____ as the brightest things on the planet.

Using any three of the singular "self" pronouns listed above, write a letter to the Ajax Candy Company asking for a job as a chocolate taster on the night shift. Tell what qualities a good employee should have, and promote yourself as a hard worker, a punctual person, and someone with "taste."

Name _____

Always Single

There are four pronouns that are always considered singular. The four pronouns are:

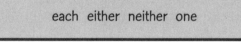

each either neither one

These four pronouns always need to be used with a singular verb. That sounds easy enough. The problem is that a prepositional phrase may confuse you by getting in the middle. Because there is a plural noun in the prepositional phrase, you may want to throw in a plural verb — even though a singular verb is correct.

How can you tell what verb goes with a singular pronoun? First leave out the prepositional phrase. Then, to see what verb goes with a singular word, substitute the word *one* for the pronoun. This sounds a lot harder than it is. Take a look at the examples below:

Examples

Each of the parrots is/are an excellent speaker. (One *is* an excellent speaker.)
Neither of the sundaes has/have fudge. (One *has* fudge.)
Either of the pies is/are acceptable. (One *is* acceptable.)
One of the alligators limp/limps. (One *limps*.)

In the above examples, the phrases *of the parrots*, *of the sundaes*, *of the pies*, and *of the alligators* may lead you to want to use a plural verb. However, the pronouns *each*, *either*, *neither* and *one* are always singular.

In the sentences below, circle the correct form of the verb.

Example

Either of them is/are ready to go.

1. Neither of us is/are brave enough to face Gertrude.

2. One of us has/have to go to the door and knock.

3. Either of us is/are capable of apologizing.

4. Each of us want/wants to, but we can't find the courage.

5. Each of the contestants has/have a bad hairdo.

6. Neither of the players likes/like practicing in the rain.

7. One of the anchorwomen always wink/winks at the end of the broadcast.

8. Either of the bull riders are/is worthy of the trophy.

9. Each of the girls wants/want to take the cruise.

10. Neither of the twirlers likes/like flaming batons.

Name _____

Everyone's Favorite

Each, *either*, *neither* and *one* are always considered singular. There are also a dozen more pronouns that require singular verbs. (These are called "indefinite" pronouns, because the nouns they stand in for are not named specifically. For example, who, exactly, is *everyone*?) These singular, indefinite pronouns are listed in the box below:

> everyone someone anyone no one
> everything something anything nothing
> everybody somebody anybody nobody

In the sentences below, circle the correct form of the verb needed in the sentence. Remember, indefinite pronouns are singular. Try substituting the word *one* for the indefinite pronoun, to see which verb form to use.

Example
> Everybody in dance class wears/wear sneakers. (One *wears* sneakers.)

1. Everyone at the dance have/has a favorite move.

2. Someone in the band does/do not play worth a dime.

3. Anyone with any brains love/loves accordion music.

4. No one in the audience listen/listens to the words.

5. Everything is/are black except for the strobe lights flickering off Rita's cast.

6. Something happen/happens each time Ruby teams up with Howard on the sax.

7. Anything goes/go when Waldo shows.

8. No one wants/want to hear Ms. Kruger play the bagpipes.

9. Everybody love/loves the way Angelo keeps time with his salad fork.

10. Somebody gag/gags every time they turn on the fog machine.

Using five of the indefinite pronouns listed above, write five sentences about any one of the following topics:

*   You attend your first meeting of the Royal Order of the Restless Mugwumps.
*   You are an alien dropped off at a mall in Detroit.
*   You attend an Italian opera with your Aunt Lilith.
*   A large tuba player faints during the Fourth of July parade.

Name _____

Pronouns of Your Own

Below is a list of singular, indefinite pronouns, and a list of prepositional phrases. Using your own paper, combine items from each list to make ten sentences that work. Make your sentences interesting. Remember that indefinite pronouns need singular verbs.

Example
    Neither of the worker bees *wants* to marry the queen.

INDEFINITE PRONOUNS
one
each
either
neither
everyone
everything
everybody
someone
something
somebody
no one
nothing
nobody
anyone
anything
anybody

PREPOSITIONAL PHRASE
of the worker bees
of the oranges
with a grain of sense
with money
by the book
in the fish tank
throughout the country
below ground
but me
of the eggplants
of the elves
of the cows
of the boys
of the girls
of the incidents
of the winners
of the losers
of the elephants
of the auctioneers
in the cellar
in her right mind

Name _____

Find Them and Fix Them

Below is a story that contains errors in grammar; some of the singular indefinite pronouns are not matched correctly with singular verbs. Find each verb that is inappropriate and cross it out. Then write in the correct verb above.

Everyone believe Bernice to be the kind of girl who finds trouble in the weirdest places. Each of her brothers are sure she won't live to graduate from high school.

For example, last year on the ski trip everybody were having fun. Someone were learning to ski for the first time, while another was taking the toughest runs with ease. Bernice, however, created a disaster. No one could believes it. Bernice missed a turn and slammed into a stretch of snow fence, taking out an entire first grade class that was playing on the bunny hill. No one were hurt, except Bernice — she was carried off the hill and into a waiting ambulance.

The following spring someone brought a pet pig to school in a cardboard box. Everybody were a little afraid of it at first and stayed back. But not Bernice. She scooped up the pig and cuddled it under her chin. She was tickling its ear when it chomped off her earring and tried to swallow it. The pig started to choke. The owner rushed it to the veterinary clinic, but it died on the way — earring overdose.

Even going to the grocery store is dangerous for Bernice, and for the store. Her mother gave her a list of produce to buy one day, so Bernice went to the supermarket. Neither of the clerks were there to help her, so she started rummaging through the broccoli on her own. One of the broccoli bunches were especially nice, but it was at the bottom of the pile. Bernice reached way over and down into the mound of bushy vegetables to get the one she wanted, when the vegetable sprayer turned on. Bernice screamed, jerked back and rammed into two stock boys carrying boxes of bananas. They were equally surprised as they fell backward into the strawberry shortcake display. As bananas flew and strawberries tumbled, Bernice scampered away with four heads of broccoli cradled in her arms. The checkout lady let her go through, free of charge, because she valued her life.

Two weeks later when no one were home, Bernice made grilled cheese sandwiches and somehow managed to melt the microwave. A week after that she washed her mom's BMW and forgot to roll up the windows. Two days later she was babysitting for the neighbors and took the children to a fast-food restaurant. She placed them in the romper gym in the kiddie room and went to order lunch. Two hours later the children still would not come out. Bernice begged them. Neither of the managers were able to coax the kids out. When Bernice tried to get at them through the emergency door, they screamed so loudly no one could stand it. Finally, the parents had to come and dig their children out from under four thousand plastic baseballs. The children said they were having too much fun to quit. Everyone else believe that the kids just didn't want to deliver themselves into the hands of the "human accident."

Name _____

Possessive Pronouns

Some pronouns have the special job of showing ownership in a sentence. These are called possessive pronouns.

Examples
    We love *our* little trips to Paris.
    Their dog ate *our* picnic.
    I enjoyed *your* comments about celery juice.
    His brother is no angel either.

People sometimes get confused with possessive pronouns. Most possessive words need an apostrophe — but not possessive pronouns. Pronouns like *hers*, *yours*, *ours*, *theirs*, and *its* do not require apostrophes. These pronouns are possessive in themselves and need no punctuation at all. Nothing. Zip. Zero.

To practice using possessive pronouns, write a brief account of a nightmare vacation you might envision taking with your family or your friends. Use at least six different possessive pronouns in your story, and don't forget details like these: ice cream cones melting all over your luggage, travelling 1,000 miles from home and meeting your math teacher in a public restroom, getting to "Reptile Acres" and finding it closed, arriving at "Waterland" with no swimsuit, sitting next to the family dog who suddenly gets carsick, etc.

| my | mine | your | yours | his | her | hers | its | our | ours | their | theirs |

_____

_____

_____

_____

_____

_____

_____

_____

_____

Name _____

Non-Sexist Pronouns

If you write, "Jasper lost his lunch," you use the pronoun *his* to refer to *Jasper*. But suppose you want to say that all the people lost their lunches. You might write, "*Everyone* lost his lunch," because you know that *everyone* is a singular indefinite pronoun that needs a singular verb. But wait a minute . . .

What about the females! Women and girls don't want to be called a *his* when they lose their lunch.

English has a problem when it comes to singular pronouns. We don't have one that means either male *or* female. So, what do you do when you have a singular indefinite pronoun like "everyone"? The old recommendation was this: Use the word *his*. *His* was said to refer to either males or females.

Well, if you followed that rule all the time, you could wind up with some pretty strange sentences, like this one: *Everyone* who is pregnant should check with *his* doctor about what foods to eat during pregnancy.

That's obviously pretty silly. Another problem is that a lot of women don't like the idea of being called *his*. "What if we used *her* instead?" they ask. "How would guys feel if they had to read sentences like this one: *Everyone* who gets a passport should have *her* birth certificate with *her*."

So — what to do? At the present time, there is no universally accepted answer. You might stick with the old rule. However, most publications nowadays instead recommend that you just try to avoid singular indefinite pronouns altogether. Instead of writing, "Everyone who wants a refund should bring his coupon," they recommend rewriting the sentence so that it reads, "People who want refunds should bring their coupons."

Another possibility is to say *his or her* instead of *his*. That is sometimes a bit awkward, but it is more accurate. Finally, another possibility is to say "their" instead of "his," which most of us do anyway in informal speech. (Example: Everyone should bring *their* umbrellas in case of rain.) Although a few publications now approve of this solution, it is not generally accepted as "proper" writing. Because *their* is plural and *everyone* is singular, your English teacher will probably *not* approve of this idea!

See if you can rewrite the sentences below so that they clearly refer to both males and females.

1. Everyone kept his cool during the food fight.

2. No one did his homework over the weekend, so everyone failed.

3. Anyone who loves his dog should avoid large, vicious cats.

4. Somebody left his dirty socks on the bus.

5. Everybody ate his fill at the taco bar.

Name _____

It's All Relative

Relative pronouns *relate* descriptive parts of a sentence to other parts of the sentence. They make messages more readable by helping words flow into a pleasant-sounding pattern. Read the messages below. Which one reads more smoothly?

- Hank ate a hot pepper. The hot pepper made him hallucinate and cry out for Rolaids.
- Hank ate a hot pepper that made him hallucinate and cry out for Rolaids.

Your ear should have told you that the second message sounds better. That is because of the hardworking relative pronoun *that*. It relates the last, descriptive part of the sentence to the word *hot pepper*.

Make each message below read more smoothly by rewriting it into one sentence, adding one of the four relative pronouns listed in the box below.

> that which whose who

1. Nobody came to the beach party. I'm talking about the beach party held in Mary's dad's garage.

   _____

2. I like mystery stories. The mystery stories I like best don't have butlers, knives, or English castles looming in the fog.

   _____

3. My teacher was a tall woman. She wore red hats and plastic shoes when she wasn't in school.

   _____

4. My neighbor once owned a cocker spaniel. It was a dog with pups that bit into their mother's ears and hung on like wood ticks.

   _____

5. Joey has a nickname. He hates the nickname.

   _____

Name _____

Pronouns Out of Place

Relative pronouns are known for being able to turn a series of sentences into one smooth sentence. However, there is a hitch. The relative pronoun always *relates* part of a sentence to the noun mentioned right before it. Here is an example:

Two young women who wore matching sundresses held identical collie puppies.

Who wore matching sundresses relates back to *women*. No problem. But look what happens if we put the relative pronoun in the wrong place:

Two young women held identical collie puppies who wore matching sundresses.

Who wore matching sundresses now relates back to *puppies*. Because the puppies weren't wearing sundresses, the sentence doesn't say what it means to say. The relative pronoun *who* needs to come right after the word it relates to — in this case, *women*.

Fix the sentences below that have been confused by the misplacement of a relative pronoun. Rewrite each sentence on the line provided.

1. The trainer turned to the crowd and said, "We need someone to jump into the tank with Boris the shark, who is absolutely odorless."

    _____

2. Julio bought cotton candy from a girl at the fair that was way too sweet.

    _____

3. I'd like to hire someone to feed and train our horse who doesn't smoke.

    _____

4. Never trust a lady with a dog who walks everywhere in high heels.

    _____

5. At the race track, I saw a horse which was oval shaped and 300 yards wide.

    _____

6. I met two men carrying smoked fish who wore chrome-plated sunglasses.

    _____

Name _____

Writing with Relatives

Using one of the four relative pronouns (*who*, *which*, *that* and *whose*), combine each set of sentences below into one sentence that reads smoothly and makes good sense.

1. This is a new flotation device. It instantly inflates to the size and shape of a St. Bernard and dog-paddles you to safety.

   _____

   _____

2. We are looking for a new photographer's assistant. This person must be able to distract children for at least 30 seconds, using distorted facial expressions.

   _____

   _____

3. Our circus needs a new act. It must have pizazz, pizoom and free balloons.

   _____

   _____

4. Across the vast distance of the Grand Canyon hung a massive black web. Everyone knew the web was the work of Spiderman.

   _____

   _____

5. The police are searching for a distraught woman. Her chimpanzee apparently stole the family car and left for St. Louis.

   _____

   _____

Interjections

What Are Interjections?

Interjections are words or short phrases that show strong emotion or surprise in a sentence; they act like crashing cymbals. Bang! The reader is suddenly alert.

Examples

Hey! Don't kill flies with my new shoes!

Yikes! That's a long way down!

Oops — I didn't see you sitting there!

Boy, am I glad to see you!

Well, I've never been so insulted in my life!

Why, I can't believe you are saying this to my face!

Interjections help us express how we feel about something. They add a dash of intensity to our everyday comments, proving that it's not just *what* we say, but *how* we say it that matters.

Name _____

All Alone in the World

Interjections are set off from the rest of the sentence with special punctuation, most often an exclamation point (!). Sometimes, however, interjections are set off from the rest of the sentence with a comma (,) or even a dash (—).

Examples

Hey! Get your hands off my lasagna!

Say — aren't you the lady who drives the ice cream truck?

Gee, I think I left my wallet in the cave.

Rewrite the sentences below, inserting the correct punctuation and capitalization. (Look at the examples above to see how it is done.) And remember, not all interjections appear at the opening of a sentence.

1. wow three large pizzas and no one is home but me

   _____

2. whoa i can't write as fast as you think

   _____

3. yikes it's hotter in here than the inside of a jalapeno pepper

   _____

4. I'm sure well actually I'm pretty sure I did it right

   _____

5. halt this is your principal speaking

   _____

6. say would you like to win a trip to Disneyland

   _____

7. great Scott your teeth have all turned yellow

   _____

Write about two friends meeting at a class reunion ten years after high school graduation. In your description, use at least three sentences with interjections.

Name _____

Hey! This Is Serious

Some people are walking interjections. Everything they say is full of drama and passion and dangerous emotion. These people could walk onto the set of a soap opera and be stars. They say things like this:

Hey! Could you lend me a pencil?
Gosh! The lead broke!
Good grief! Could you loan me another one!
Seriously! Could you lend me another pencil?
Holy cow! You're my best friend!

Using the interjections listed below, and any of your own you would like to throw in, write a ten-sentence dialogue between yourself and an interjection user. The situation should be an ordinary event that is made bigger than life (more important than it really is) by the person you are talking to. Have fun. Be weird. And borrow a pencil if you need one!

> hey geez gosh say aha ha yes no oh
> oops bravo well what now so sure why

_____

_____

_____

_____

_____

_____

_____

_____

_____

_____

_____

_____

Name _____

Holy Bat Wings!

An interjection is an expression of strong emotion. But all expressions of emotion don't have to be serious. In fact, in the television show *Batman*, crime fighter Robin uses a collection of goofy and humorous interjections. He will say things like, "Holy spider webs! It's that malicious fiend, Black Widow!" or "Suffering Stalactites! This cave is lined with super-repellent Bat-foil!"

On the lines below, write some sentences that use a ridiculous interjection at the opening. You may create several sentences about one topic or situation, or you may write a random collection of sentences on a variety of subjects.

Examples
  Holy hubcaps! The car won't start!
  Jumpin' jelly beans! It's Easter morning!

1. _____

2. _____

3. _____

4. _____

5. _____

6. _____

7. _____

8. _____

9. _____

10. _____

Adverbs

✳ CAREFULLY SLOWLY TOO SOMEWHERE ✳

ANYWHERE DARINGLY

VERY CALMLY SHYLY

What Are Adverbs?

✳ OFTEN HERE THERE NEVER NOT SOON ✳

You can tell what adverbs do just by listening to their name. Adverbs *add to verbs*. They give us more information about *how, where, when* or *to what extent* the action of the verb is being performed.

For example, you could say, "Louise stirred the mashed potatoes." Or you could say, "Louise stirred the mashed potatoes *menacingly*." (In other words, look out!) *Menacingly* is an adverb that tells us *how* Louise stirred. It adds to the meaning of the verb.

All that sounds pretty easy, but it gets a bit more complicated. Adverbs give us more information about two other kinds of words, besides verbs: adjectives and other adverbs.

If you write, "The salami sandwich was amazingly delicious," you are telling us *how* delicious it was. *Amazingly* is an adverb that gives us added information about the adjective *delicious*.

If you write, "Mr. Keith rather tactfully insulted the other coach," you are telling *how* tactfully he insulted. *Rather* is an adverb giving added information about another adverb.

Here are three hints to help you recognize adverbs:

- They often end in *ly*.
- The words *very* and *too* are probably the most common adverbs.
- The words *never* and *not* are usually adverbs.

Name _____

Adverbs? How?

Adverbs often answer the question, "How?" They give more information about verbs, adjectives or other adverbs. Look at the examples below. Each adverb has an arrow pointing to the verb, adjective or adverb it is giving added information about.

Examples

Bernice was terribly mean to Dwight during the holidays. (How mean? Terribly mean.)

Wayne's parrot has a very scary face. (How scary? Very scary.)

The frog sat perfectly still as the snake slithered toward it. (How still? Perfectly still.)

Each of the sentences below contains an adverb. Draw an arrow from the adverb to the verb, adjective or adverb it gives added information about.

1. Jane smiled wickedly at the sound of Alonzo's footsteps on the porch.

2. Alphonse used to own an incredibly lazy Siamese cat.

3. Juan tore anxiously at the wrapping on the long, heavy box.

4. April quickly inserted the breath mint under her tongue.

5. Chen cautiously slipped the key from the lock and turned the rusty knob.

6. Elaine carefully stashed the peanut butter cups in her top drawer.

7. Glen reached desperately for the plunger.

8. His badly cut hair went unnoticed at the dance.

9. Woo's goldfish slowly nibbled the worm to pieces.

10. Allan completely ignores his hunger pangs until he gets off the bus.

Add your own adverbs to the sentences below:

• Elizabeth faced the dangerous enemy.
• Melanie examined her haircut and bawled.
• A tornado descended upon the town and tore it apart.

Name _____

Adverbs? Where?

Besides telling you *how* something is done, adverbs can tell you *where* it is done.

Examples
>   Help! Somebody help! She's going *under* for the third time! (Going where? Under.)
>   Her hair was combed *up* into an ice cream cone swirl. (Combed where? Up.)
>   Come *back*, Toto! Come back! (Come where? Back.)

Choose adverbs from those in the box below to help tell *where* in the sentences below. Use each adverb only once, writing it on the line provided.

> in out up down around back forward behind there to

1. If all the passengers will lean_____, it will reduce the chance of an immediate crash.

2. If you sit _____ doing this all day, you'll drive me, your mother and the dog nuts!

3. You should have left your guilt _____ when you moved out here.

4. "We can't go _____ now," Mike said. "The elephant's dead!"

Using five "where" adverbs, write the directions for a treasure map that tells your teacher where to find the restroom pass that the class "accidentally" hid somewhere in the school.

_____

_____

_____

_____

_____

_____

_____

_____

The Case of the Adverb Clue

Some adverbs slip into a sentence, and you hardly know they are there (like the adverb *there*, for example.) Other adverbs tell you in neon lights, "Yo! Hey! Check this out — I'm an adverb!" These brassy adverbs carry the word *where* right in their names:

> somewhere   nowhere   everywhere   anywhere   elsewhere

Choose one of these five "where" adverbs to complete each sentence below.

1. "If you don't change your attitude, you are going _____ in this business," Ricky's manager said.

2. "I can book a concert _____ in this country!" Ricky replied.

3. "I've got friends _____ ," he added.

4. "Someday you're going to meet somebody _____ who'll take you down a notch or two," Ricky's manager threatened.

5. "I'm going somewhere else," Ricky said.
   "Don't you mean, in proper English, _____ ?" Ricky's manager retorted as he stomped out of the room.

Using five "where" adverbs in your sentences, describe how six kids got lost on a science field trip and spent the night in the woods along Lake Minirumpus.

_____

_____

_____

_____

_____

_____

_____

_____

Name _____

Adverbs? When?

Adverbs not only tell you how and where something is done, they tell when.

Examples

I sold my first tricycle *yesterday*. (Sold it when? Yesterday.)
Whenever I'm blue, I think of you. (I think of you when? Whenever I'm blue.)
I'll *always* remember the time you ate that raw squid. (Remember when? Always.)
Before you open your mouth, consider the consequences. (Consider when? Before you open your mouth.)

The ten "time" adverbs listed below tell when something has happened, is happening, or will happen. Choose one that is appropriate for each of the ten sentences, and write the adverb on the line provided.

> sometime someday never eventually suddenly
> after before until immediately later

1. Billie's mom believed with all her heart that _____ she and Billie would sit down over a nice green salad, and talk.

2. Pablo looked at his plate and said, "I _____ met a hamburger I didn't like."

3. Margaret's favorite dream was to be on the cover of a diet book in one of those dramatic -and-after photos.

4. Thu Li said, "See you _____ alligator."
   William replied, "After while, crocodile."

5. _____ Eleanor got used to the python's habit of entwining itself around the garden hose.

6. It was a stormy night at sea. _____ Sam Blackhawk realized he was not alone on the cruise ship.

Write three sentences that use "when" adverbs to tell about a family event that you absolutely hated from the minute you arrived until the minute you left (Grandma's birthday, the family reunion at Lake Towanda, a 50th wedding anniversary, etc.).

Name _____

Adverbs? To What Extent?

Some adverbs don't tell how, when, or where. They tell "to what extent" or "to what degree" something happens.

For example, you could say, "Joanne hates me." Or you could say, "Joanne *almost* hates me."

The adverb *almost* hints of a certain complexity in the relationship between Joanne and you. To what degree does Joanne hate you? The verb *almost*, as it is used here, makes the message of the sentence more intriguing.

Using the adverbs listed below, write five sentences of your own that build some suspense.

> rather   somewhat   largely   clearly   quite

1. _____

_____

2. _____

_____

3. _____

_____

4. _____

_____

5. _____

_____

Name _____

Adverbs . . . Not Just for Verbs Anymore

Adverbs add information about verbs. They also do the same for adjectives and other adverbs.

For example, you could use the adverb *always* to describe the adjective *mean*: "Bernice was *always mean* to Dwight during the holidays." Or, you could use the adverb *always* to describe the adverb *terribly*: "Bernice was *always terribly* mean to Dwight during the holidays."

The sentences below use adverbs to add information about verbs, adjectives and other adverbs. Draw a circle around each adverb. Draw an arrow to the verb, adjective or adverb it gives information about.

Examples

Agnes counts her chickens very carefully before they are hatched.
Hadleyville is delightfully beautiful on the night before Christmas.

1. Judy's dog has a very ferocious bark.

2. Jubal said, "I can't love a girl I never have seen!"

3. Jane's dad cut the cake into ridiculously tiny pieces.

4. The car was so thoroughly rusted that Billy's lunch fell through a hole in the floor and was quickly lost along Highway 30.

5. Darlene was moving dangerously close to the plate of burritos at the end of the counter.

6. Pedro entered the room and gave a completely fake smile to everyone at the table.

7. Hippos would get more respect if they weren't so awkwardly built.

8. Edward eventually gave away every cent he had won.

Write three sentences using adverbs to describe how Elaine Hidalgo got locked into her seat on the ride called "The Bullet" at the carnival and hung upside down for the entire afternoon.

_____

_____

_____

_____

_____

_____

_____

Name _____

Lights! Action! Adverbs!

You are a movie mogul who has five new releases coming out next year, each with a title that is exciting and intriguing — and which contains at least one adverb. You are aware that films like *Always*, *Forever Young*, *Never Cry Wolf*, and *Living Dangerously* all have adverbs in their titles. However, you want your titles to be even more alluring to crowds with movie money rattling around in their pockets.

Below, invent four separate movie titles of your own. Then write a brief description of each film, using at least ten adverbs altogether. Circle every adverb you use. Try to create titles and movies with some variety: a love story, an action film, a horror movie and a Western, for example. Be wild. Be creative. And don't forget the adverbs!

1. Title: _____

   Description: _____

   _____

   _____

2. Title: _____

   Description: _____

   _____

   _____

3. Title: _____

   Description: _____

   _____

4. Title: _____

   Description: _____

   _____

   _____

Name _____

Tagging Along

Tag lines are used when writing dialogue. The tag line is the part of the quotation that tells who spoke and how they spoke.

"Come here!" *Wilt said.*
"No!" *Herbert replied.*

Have some fun with tag lines in the exercise below. Add an adverb from the box to each tag line, making an adverb pun.

Examples
"This knife is dull!" the butcher said *sharply.*
"You light up my life," the firefly said *glowingly.*

> haltingly fittingly hollowly slowly quizzically
> dramatically speedily aimlessly sheepishly flatly

1. "Go fix the tire," the mechanic said _____.

2. "That suit looks perfect on you," the tailor said _____.

3. "Are we ready for our test?" the teacher asked _____.

4. "This will be a sad performance," said the playwright _____.

5. "Would you all please wait for little old me?" the snail said _____.

6. "I'm ashamed to be part of this herd," said the ewe _____.

7. "I think — I really think — we should stop this train," the brakeman said _____.

8. "Alas, I will never be a real boy," said the hand puppet _____.

9. "I wish I could hit the bull's-eye," the marksman said _____.

10. "I'm the one who took home the trophy," said the runner _____.

Now write at least five wacky adverb tag lines of your own.

Name _____

Adverb Overflow

Adverbs can be useful, like ice cubes in a punch bowl. However, too many can water down your message until it is meaningless.

Read the summary below of the film *Beauty and the Beast*. Then rewrite the summary in your own words, eliminating the adverbs that are, in your opinion, overdone, unnecessary and downright useless.

Beauty and the Beast is the story of a *rather* intelligent, *rather* dreamy-headed girl named Belle, who lives in a *rather* small village with her aging father, who is a *somewhat* fumbling inventor. He spends all day creating *quite* strange machines that *fairly often* don't work.

One day he decides to travel to the fair to demonstrate his latest invention, but he gets *rather* lost on the way. He walks to the *quite* creepy castle of the Beast, who traps the old man in a *quite* nasty prison. Belle *hurriedly* comes looking for her father and *quickly* exchanges herself for her father, who is *rather* ill. The Beast treats her *somewhat badly* at first, but he *eventually* falls *deeply* in love with her.

Meanwhile she learns of the *simply* incredible legend surrounding the *rather* lonely beast. He must be loved *truly* and *simply* by someone in order for the *terribly* awful spell of ugliness to be broken. Belle *eventually* learns to love him *enormously*, but not before the Beast's castle is stormed and the *horribly* jealous character Gaston *viciously* stabs the Beast, *fatally* wounding him. The Beast *bravely* shoves Gaston to his death, then *promptly* gasps his last *incredibly* long breath and dies. Belle kisses him, and the Beast comes to life and is transformed into an *unbelievably* handsome prince. Belle and the Prince live *totally, completely, happily ever after*.

_____

_____

_____

_____

_____

_____

_____

_____

_____

_____

_____

Name _____

Party Time

Describe the dullest party in teenage history. In your description, use at least five adverbs from the box below.

Here are a few facts about this party, to get you started:

* The dining room table is set with glasses of buttermilk.
* Orchestra music wafts from the stereo like a bad odor.
* Nobody is allowed to hold hands.
* Everyone is asked to use quiet "inside" voices.

> unbelievably incredibly awfully very never quite somewhat terribly
> endlessly badly slowly anxiously cleverly stupidly numbly hysterically
> absolutely completely foolishly unbearably angrily nervously surely

_____

_____

_____

_____

_____

_____

_____

_____

_____

_____

_____

_____

Answer Keys

Answer Key
Five Hundred Horsepower, page 12

1. weaseled, cursed
2. kneaded, wished
3. pounded, demanded
4. snapped, stuck
5. peered
6. snickered, tiptoed
7. hurled, plopped
8. spit

The dog and cat **gripped** each other's paws as they **plunged** over the edge of the cliff into the stunt net below.
Henry **jerked** the cap off the soda bottle and it exploded.
The chemistry teacher **sashayed** up to the health teacher and **asked** her to dance with him.
As Mick **bowed**, his toupee **slid** to the floor, and the audience **howled**.
Alfredo **tumbled** head over heels into the trash cans.

Answer Key
Verb Variety, page 13

Build a snowman	bend, roll, pack, lift, stack, pat, smooth, insert, dress, photograph, admire
Throw a party	decorate, sweep, invite, wax, dust, rearrange, buy, bake, dance, yawn, sleep
Fly a kite	tie, tighten, tug, pull, run, reel, gaze, drag, jerk, laugh
Make a banana split	dip, scoop, open, slice, thaw, spray, slurp, lick, smile, burp
Clean your room	lift, stash, stuff, bury, wipe, wash, scrap, fluff, sort, find, hide, lock, leave

Answer Key
Verbs Alive, page 14

1. Philip **crooned** . . .
   Elizabeth **screamed**, "Then buy me some jade flatware!"
2. you've **created** . . .
   Rashad **snarled**, "Don't toy with me, Louise!"
3. and **gnawed** off . . .
   Alvin **shrieked**, "Get this man some Tums!"

4. The beauty queen **marched** . . .
   "Consider me fired," she **sneered**.
5. Paula **jerked** . . .
   "I hate anything made of polyester," she **whined**.
6. Walter **stumbled** . . .
   "I'm a goner," he **moaned**, and closed his eyes for the last time.
7. The pigeon **slouched** . . .
   He remembered **scrounging** french fries at the drive-in with his old buddy.

Answer Key
Pop Goes the Verb, page 15

Sample answer, with only the more lively verbs bolded.

I never thought it would come to this. When I was just a little can — the size they give you on airplanes — I had big dreams. I thought one day I might **rise** to stardom, maybe even **star** in a commercial or **refresh** the thirst of a big NFL player during the Super Bowl. But then those yuppie little sport drinks **arrived** on the scene, and nobody wanted soda anymore. I guess you could say I was canned. I ended up as part of just another twelve pack.

Some kid **popped** my top off, **guzzled** my soda and **burped**. Then he dropped me down in the grass and **sauntered** away. I **rusted** in the rain for three days before some guy **crunched** me flat with the heel of his boot and **slung** me in a trash bag. Luckily I managed to **tear** a hole in the bag and **slip** out before I was **crushed** even smaller and then **ground** up at the recycling center.

But life is still hard. I've been **slammed** around the street like a hockey puck, **launched** into the air like a boomerang and **slapped** on the river, like a stone. Will it never end?

Answer Key
Catastrophic Verbs, page 16

Sample answer, with only the more lively verbs bolded.

If tornadoes had names, the one that hit rural Oklahoma Saturday afternoon would surely be called "Total Devastation." In only three minutes, the tornado completely **flattened** the small community of Okey Dokey.

The twister first **touched** down at 3:10 P.M., **ripping** the roof off Dalyrimples' Shoe Store. Reeboks and Nikes **flew** down the street, spinning in the twister's 90 mile an hour winds. Within minutes, the twister **pummeled** City Hall and splintered the bandstand in the city park.

As the twister **thundered** down the road, terrified residents **screamed** and **scurried** for cover. Store fronts **collapsed**, park benches **tumbled**, and bicycle racks **screeched** down the center of the street.

After just three minutes, the tornado **withdrew** into the clouds, leaving the stunned citizens of Okey Dokey to **cope** with the devastation it left behind.

Answer Key
The Ls Have It, page 17

On Saturday morning, the citizens of Garland, Kansas, gathered in the field north of town to await the arrival of Dr. Dee and his hot air balloon. National television reporters, who **loathed** small-town events, **leered** at each other. The townspeople **lounged** on the ground eating. They had **loaded** their cars with hot dogs, portable grills and coolers full of pop and beer. Dr. Dee's hot air balloon journey across the United States was national news and the scheduled stop in Garland was cause for celebration.

As Dr. Dee's balloon appeared in the sky about 2:00 P.M., Mayor Young and all six city council members **linked** their arms together and put on their specially-designed hats with letters that spelled WELCOME. Picnickers **leapt** to their feet and waved. As the balloon floated closer, Dr. Dee **leaned** over the edge of the basket and waved to the crowd. Unfortunately, as the balloon landed, it **lurched** toward the excited crowd. The mayor and the entire city council, lined up in front of the crowd, were knocked to the ground. The mayor **limped** to the balloon but fell just as he reached Dr. Dee.

We learned later that the mayor's ankle was broken in three places and he'll be on crutches for six weeks. During an interview from his bed, the mayor remarked, "How I **longed** to be the first to greet Dr. Dee."

During Dr. Dee's one-hour stay in Garland, he ate four hot dogs, a bowl of potato salad and drank three beers. He then left Garland and headed his balloon for Chicago.

Answer Key
Time Warp, page 18

Last summer my mother agreed to let me take horseback-riding lessons. I signed up at a dude ranch outside of our town. I had never been close to a horse before but had seen people riding horses on television and in the movies. I was sure it would be easy.

The first problem I had was just getting on the horse. The instructor showed me how to boost myself into the saddle. I grabbed the reins and held on to the saddle horn. After a half hour of riding, my legs ached and my hands were stiff from clutching the reins.

When the first lesson was over, I was happy to get down from the horse and go home. I thought about quitting, but since my mom had paid for six lessons, I went back the next week. This time, I got on by myself, relaxed my hands on the reins and looked around as the horse walked. It started to be fun. After the second lesson I couldn't wait to come back.

I loved riding horses. I really enjoyed being outside, and the horse I rode acted like he knew me. Best of all, I learned not to quit something after just one attempt. My mom kept telling me this, but I had to learn it myself.

Answer Key
Tight Connections, page 19

1. "I **have been** thinking, Billy."
2. "What **have** you **been** thinking?"
3. "I **have been** thinking we ought to sell water balloons as a business."
4. "You **are** kidding! **Should** we sell them with water, or without?"
5. "We **should** sell them full of water, Billy. I **am** not one to cheat my customers."

Answer Key
Setting the Scene, page 20

The pencil trembled in her fingers. The answers wouldn't come. She gripped harder as her mind searched. Her heart pounded. Her throat contracted. She squinted her eyes, trying to squeeze the answer out. Her cheeks dampened. What was it? She sighed. She looked around. She bit her lip. She allowed her eyes to wander the room. Then she focused on her desk, staring at the peeling edges. She chewed on her pencil. Her eyes glazed over. Her mind was blank.

Answer Key
Rewriting Mother Goose, page 21

Sample answer, with only the more lively verbs bolded.

Once there was a man named Jack who **swore** up and down that he definitely, without any doubt, could not eat fat. He **claimed** it was a digestive problem he had had since birth. Because he lived in a ranching community, his refusal to eat fat was a very big deal. The townspeople **scolded** and **whined** and **acted** disgusted with him.

Jack **wasted** a lot of food, not eating fat. Then one day in the grocery store as Jack was **wandering** along carefully **examining** the celery and cauliflower, he accidentally **rammed** his cart into a beautiful woman selecting radishes. Their eyes met. They **locked**. She **smiled**. He **blushed**. They did the rest of their shopping together that day. That's how he found out the woman's secret: She survived on vegetables and fat cut from the meat she bought. She **loved** fat. Perfect! Now those grumpy townspeople could stop **whining** about how much food he **wasted**. Jack knew in an instant that this was the woman for him. He knew that, together, they would **lick** the platter clean.

Answer Key
On a Clear Noun You Can See Forever, page 26

Kodiak, a huge Saint Bernard, bounded onto the playground and knocked over five kindergartners with his tail.
A trapeze artist hurled herself into the circus elephants' water trough and dragged the toddler out of the fodder and algae.
The two Boy Scouts devoured a two-layer chocolate mint cake, three packages of wieners and half a bucket of leftover Kentucky Fried Chicken.

Answer Key
Common Nouns and Proper Nouns, page 27

1. At McNichols Arena I cheered for the Denver Nuggets.
2. Paula's Porsche convertible was far more expensive than our Dodge Caravan.
3. I visited the Hard Rock Cafe on Friday last week.
4. Meg got Calvin Klein jeans, Nikes and a Faith Hill CD for her birthday.

Answer Key
Replace Dead Nouns, page 28

1. My little sister climbed the fence and turned loose every Doberman in Doggy Land.
2. Mr. Langston's cockatoo, Manny, insulted Reverend Goddard from the First Baptist Church.
3. During a chemistry lecture, Mr. Vincent accidentally rubbed chalk all over his chin and the tip of his large nose.
4. Raphael, the chef at Smithy's, uses leftover linguini to create tasty snacks for his little terrier, Max.
5. Bart hit a goat with his Harley Davidson.
6. My neighbor Justine's 1972 station wagon blew up last night.

Answer Key,
Muckberry Gazette, page 29

BM3 train derails
The BM3 commuter train derailed today on its way to Pleasantville, injuring seven Sunshine Girls from Troop #209 and five troop leaders. Four monkeys bound for the Big Top Circus were also injured when a Volvo, a Honda and Gremlin collided with the train's caboose as it tipped over. City Manager Donna Nicklos said the accident was being cleaned up by volunteers from the Muckberry Emergency Response Association. Muckberryites are asked to stay away from the wreckage until noon on Thursday.

Answer Key,
More Muckberry, page 30

Well-known archaeologist Lily Leakston and two other scientists, Gerome Clancy and Jethro Manahan, have stumbled onto the eggs of a Horuptosaurus, a rare dinosaur believed to have roamed the dry regions of Nevada 65 million years ago. Leakston and her colleagues insist that Muckberry University should receive the specimens and begin testing for signs of life soon.

Two adolescent females were seen entering Sally Grugen's Grocery, the only grocery store in Pleasantville, yesterday at approximately 2:00 P.M. Soon after, the youngsters were observed fleeing the store with two stolen potatoes and a bag of tortillas. Officers John Johnson and James Jamison have asked that anyone with information on the suspects call them at 555-8123.

Sally Grugen appeared on local station KCOD yesterday evening, offering a tearful plea for the return of her potatoes and tortillas. "I hope they find these juvenile delinquents and lock them up forever!" she said. "Now I can't trust anyone anymore!"

Answer Key,
Be Sharp, page 31

Chaos reigned over Muckberry late Thursday night as a fire in Freddie's Firework Factory caused fireworks to explode in the dark sky. The unintentional fireworks display occurred at 11:15 p.m., leaving 12 factory workers injured. No one can explain the cause of the fire that set off everything from Roman candles to sparklers, but investigators are searching around the clock for clues.

Anita Barrows, 79, who lives across the street from the factory, was home when the explosion of fireworks occurred. "I was watching 'Gunsmoke' when I heard the loud whistles of fireworks shooting up into the air and firecrackers going 'Boom! Boom! Boom!' At first I thought the thunderous noise was coming from my television, but I soon realized that it was not. I stepped outside and narrowly missed being hit by flying blue and red sparks! I didn't know what was happening, but it was a beautiful sight nonetheless."

Other eyewitnesses said when they heard the explosions, they went outside to investigate and ended up being treated to a lovely scene of fireworks in the sky. Avery Kidder, 19, was walking home past the factory when the fireworks began exploding. "First I heard a hiss and then I saw a beam of green light shoot up into the sky and arc. After that there was a loud 'Bang!' and I just stood there, mesmerized. It ended up being a pretty good display of fireworks, even though it was pretty unlucky for the factory owners and workers."

The names of the 12 injured factory workers have not yet been released. They have been taken to St. Dominick's Hospital for treatment.

Answer Key,
What's the Dif?, page 32

1.	mild:	perspiration	6.	harsh:	guts	11.	harsh:	slammer
	harsh:	sweat		mild:	courage		mild:	prison
2.	mild:	cabin	7.	harsh:	pimple	12.	mild:	informer
	harsh:	shack		mild:	blemish		harsh:	snitch
3.	mild:	debris	8.	mild:	alcohol	13.	mild:	dirt
	harsh:	trash		harsh:	booze		harsh:	filth
4.	mild:	news	9.	harsh:	war	14.	harsh:	mess
	harsh:	gossip		mild:	conflict		mild:	trouble
5.	harsh:	job	10.	mild:	underarm	15.	harsh:	dump
	mild:	career		harsh:	armpit		mild:	landfill

Ten original noun pairs

1. converse
   yak
2. group
   gang
3. eccentric
   nut
4. celebration
   bash
5. juvenile
   kid
6. soil
   dirt
7. altercation
   fight
8. film
   flick
9. admirer
   fan
10. vehicle
    car

Answer Key, Leaving Home, page 33

Dear Mom and Dad,

   I hope you are doing well. How are you enjoying the garage? I am so glad I was able to clean it for you before I left. Boy, was it a mess!

   Well, Jerry and I are getting along well. I'm sure you've heard he's getting married and would like me to attend the wedding in Brazil. Of course, I would love to go, but you know how it is when you have to be a responsible adult. I have to pay the phone bill, the gas bill, the water bill, the credit card bill and the rent. Things are going okay, though. Food can be a little scarce sometimes. I eat a lot of Budget Noodles. All I have to do is add hot water. That is sometimes a little difficult when, every once in a while, the gas gets turned off. But even then I can heat the water over our Ever-Heat halogen lamp. Those things put out a lot of heat, so you won't have to worry about me freezing to death this winter. I am so grateful you guys taught me to be so resourceful! How would I do it without you?

   I hope I didn't worry you with that comment about freezing to death this winter. Just to put your minds at ease, I have thought of another way to make completely sure I survive the winter. Lucky for us, Jerry's wedding will be in Brazil, right on the banks of the Amazon — it's *very* warm there. If you let me borrow money to go to Brazil for a few weeks this winter, there would be absolutely no danger of my freezing to death in Chicago. I've got to run. There's a guy from the electric company at the door.

   Hope to hear from you soon!
Love,
Your shivering son, Michael

Answer Key
In the Beginning, page 38

1. "The sky is getting dark **toward** the east."
2. "It may rain **on** us."
3. "We should take cover **before** we get wet."
4. "We might hide **in** a cave."
5. "No. We should climb a tree and hide **among** the leaves."
6. "I can't. I'm afraid **of** heights."
7. "Before we were married you weren't afraid **of** heights."
8. "I'd rather crawl **into** a hole."
9. "You are afraid **of** the dark."
   "In fact, you are afraid **of** everything."
10. "I am not afraid **of** you."

Og said to Ug, "If you're not afraid **of** me, come with me **to** those trees. We'll take shelter **beneath** the branches."

So Ug walked **behind** Og **to** the trees where they stayed **under** the canopy **of** leaves. They sat and watched the rain fall **from** the sky and kept warm and dry **until** the storm ended.

"I'm hungry; let's go get some grub," said Ug.

"You must wait **until** I go hunting," said Og.

"I can't wait that long," said Ug. "Let's just sit here **under** these trees and eat some leaves."

"You're too impatient," said Og. "You can't wait **for** anything."

"Not true," said Ug. "I waited **for** you."

Answer Key
Cleaning Up, page 39

1. on, of, with
2. over
3. within, into, of, upon
4. for
5. at, for
6. across, over, of, onto, in
7. for
8. of
9. of

Answer Key
Catching the Drift, page 40

1. Nobody **in** my family has a nose **like** my dad's.
2. Whenever I'm **at** Jennifer's house, I always start to sneeze.
3. Take the knife out **of** that toaster, or you'll light up **like** a Christmas tree!
4. Anyone **with** any sense takes an extra pair of shoes along when camping **in** the mountains.
5. **By** the time I reached Andrew, he was plastered **with** artichoke dip.
6. I ran **up** the stairs **to** the bathroom and slammed the door **on** my foot.
7. **Without** money, there is no reason to go shopping.
8. Always jog **in** the morning; it's cooler, and no one sees you **in** those strange outfits.

Answer Key
The Correct Preposition, Please, page 41

1. I was never anywhere **near** the chase because I was busy feeding the homeless.
2. I pretended to throw the diamonds **into** the fire, but I really gave them back to their rightful owners.
3. I was **in** the basement **under** the dorm playing Nintendo.
4. I ran **into** the pole just **before** the officer yelled, "Halt!"
5. Actually, I was standing **upon** his head.
6. I checked the oven several times **throughout** the robbery because I wasn't going to let any criminal ruin my Bundt cake.
7. The jury finds **against** the defendant because no one believes his excuse about psychological abuse.

Answer Key
Unnecessary Prepositions, page 42

1. When do I have to return it?
2. Where are we in the story?
3. Why are you hanging around?
4. Everyone but John is finished.
5. Where will you be sitting when I come into the theater?
6. Where did you buy that interesting green blouse?
7. I can't figure out where Jolene goes every Tuesday afternoon.
8. You shouldn't have gotten us into all this trouble.
9. Tell me where you put my radio.
10. Where is your brother heading?

Answer Key
Prepositions in Concert, page 44

1. in Kansas
2. in your slippers
3. on him/like a ton/of bricks
4. in business
5. without Toto
6. The munchkins danced (in a circle).
7. The wicked witch (of the west) scared Dorothy.
8. Dorothy's friends were standing (around her bed) as she awoke.
9. The wizard's balloon disappeared (into the sky).
10. The wizard performed magic tricks (behind the curtain).

Answer Key
Professional Phrases, page 45

A Farewell to Arms: In the late summer; of that year; in a house; in a village; across the river and the plain; to the mountains; in the bed; of the river; in the sun; in the channels; by the house; down the road; of the trees

All Quiet on the Western Front: at rest; behind the front; of beef and haricot beans; at peace; for the evening; of sausage and bread; in fine trim; for a long time

The Good Earth: At first; in the blackness; of the curtains; about his bed; from any other; except for the faint, gasping cough; of his old father; to his own; across the middle room

The Slave Dancer: In a hinged, wooden box; upon the top; of which; of her trade; with my finger; from the poorhouse; with enough food

Charlotte's Web: with that ax; to her mother; for breakfast; to the hoghouse; of the pigs; to anything; with it

Jolen looked at the box **for a long time**.

Linda knew the night would not be different **from any other Christmas**.

"Don't chop wood **with that axe**," cried Uncle Ralph.

Her mother cooked up a bunch **of sausage and bread for breakfast**.

In the blackness, Emily tried to find a candle.

It was quiet **except for the faint gasping cough of the pigs in a hinged, wooden box by the house**.

Answer Key
Make Your Own, page 46

1. Erika was **under suspicion for the Great Chocolate Potato Chip Heist** because **of the unusual outbreak of pimples on her face**.
2. Wendy called the wedding off **on Wednesday** when she realized Walter was not the man **of her dreams**.
3. "**Before tomorrow**," Phil's mother warned, "you need to have cleaned the litter-box, eaten your succotash and finished all **of your homework**."
4. Molly knew she would be **in trouble** when her older sister Dena discovered the mysterious blue streak **on the seat of her favorite pink gabardine pants**.
5. **During Christmas break**, I will rewrite all **of history with my new recipe for death-defying fruitcake**.
6. Francis knew he couldn't pretend to love Felicia **throughout winter**, so he made plans to break up **with her before Valentine's Day**.
7. **Against all odds**, I will train my gerbils to swim the breaststroke **by Halloween**.
8. **In the darkness of the Sadie Hawkins luau**, Sabrina mistakenly thought Ralph was cute.
9. When Dylan adopted his Chihuahua **from the pound**, he was determined to teach this sad puppy a little **about joy and love**.
10. Rita returned Ryan's class ring, his letter jacket and his Hanson CD and chose to live her life **without him**.

Answer Key
Pick Your Preposition, page 47

Between you and me, between is my favorite preposition. In the summer, I stand between my brother Jake and the electric fan so I can cool off first. When he complains, I place a door between his whines and my mother's ear so that she can't hear him tattling. Later, to make up to him, I hide a peanut butter and jelly sandwich between his mattress and his pillow so when he gets hungry in the night, he doesn't have to go to the kitchen. We squeeze the air out from between us when we hug in the morning.

Answer Key
Phrases from the Dark Side, page 48

Across town, just before midnight, a wail like the scream of a coyote sliced the silent night air. I sat up in bed, shaking from head to foot. I sleep by the window and don't know whether it was fear or the cold that made me shiver.

Awake, I concentrated on any other unusual sounds that fell upon my ear. I thought about the space between the stairs and the doorway and wondered if it was large enough to hide an intruder, waiting under the stairs until my family went to bed.

With these thoughts circling in my head, I almost missed the sound of wet boots in the slimy muck under my bedroom window. I threw off my covers, hopped out of bed, ran straight to my parents' room and dove under their covers.

My father was missing! I crept to the garden. It was very dark, but I was able to see among the cabbages the form of a hulking creature weighing around 600 pounds.

I screamed. This was the end. Then I began to recognize certain creature features: the handlebar mustache, the wagging tail, the striped pajama bottoms, the wet black nose.

The creature was Dad holding Ralphie, our poodle! "Ralphie has been in a fight with a skunk," said Dad.

I ran to the house, holding my nose.

Answer Key
Here's . . . the Adjective!, page 52

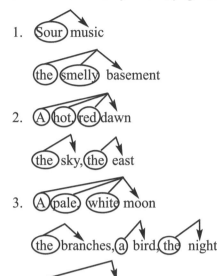

1. Sour music

   the smelly basement

2. A hot red dawn

   the sky, the east

3. A pale white moon

   the branches, a bird, the night

4. cold french fries

   (Note: *French fries* and *ice cream* are generally considered to be two-word nouns.)

5. Black hate

   the crumpled car

   (Note: Depending on preference, *his* may be considered a possessive pronoun or an adjective.)

Answer Key
Jazzing It Up, page 53

I hate camping and hiking and all those outdoor activities that include insects and sweating and climbing and sleeping on the ground. But my dad promised to go backpacking with my brother and his two weird friends, and he said he couldn't leave me alone. So, I spent a miserable, sleepless night in a smelly sleeping bag.

After an exhausting five-mile hike up a steep, winding trail through a damp, mosquito-infested forest, we finally stopped and set up camp in a clearing at the top of a colossal hill. The boys had planned the menu, and supper consisted of burnt hot dogs on dry buns, greasy potato chips, chocolate bars and grape juice. After this disgusting meal, I crawled into my sleeping bag and tried to digest. It was going to be an uncomfortable, miserable night.

My stomach churned and gurgled while I watched the stars disappear behind large thunderclouds. As the first few raindrops plunked onto my forehead, I whimpered softly, knowing no one within ten miles would hear me. I pulled the sleeping bag over my head and tried to imagine myself sleeping in a dry bed under a white fluffy comforter in my pink and white bedroom with the rose-covered wallpaper. Morning was still many hours away.

1. f   7. a or d
2. k   8. c
3. b   9. h
4. g   10. i
5. l   11. j
6. d   12. e

1. Cake decorator trying to explain an error to a bride: I hope you are not **upset** that I accidentally wrote the name Dolores on the cake instead of Gladys, since I just got your cake confused with the Happy Retirement cake I was decorating.
   Student explaining why the teacher can't flunk him: Mrs. Risenhover, if you flunk me, my parents will be **hysterical** and most likely will not buy me the new skis I need for this winter.

2. An interior decorator talking to a customer: Mrs. Birroteau, I do appreciate the discriminating taste of a **particular** client.
   Same interior decorator talking to co-workers: Mrs. Birroteau is nothing but a **fussy** snob who has nothing to do but make my life miserable.

3. Husband answering wife's questions: Well, honey, maybe you are just the tiniest bit **overweight**.
   Aerobics instructor getting her class to work harder: Lift those knees higher, or you are all going to wind up being **fat**.

4. Babysitter reporting to some parents: Jeff started out the day being rather **unpleasant**, but it was nothing a nap couldn't solve.
   Babysitter reporting to other parents: I wouldn't care if you paid me $20 an hour; I will never ever baby sit your **bratty** kid again.

5. Dentist talking to a new patient: Of course we will work together to try to prevent tooth **decay**.
   Dentist trying to convince a difficult patient to brush her teeth: Mrs. Pratt, you cannot go another five years without brushing your teeth, since they are completely **rotting** out of your head.

6. Waiter talking to customers: If you are interested in our more **inexpensive** entrees, I could always bring you the children's menu.
   Girl breaking up with her boyfriend: I'm returning this **cheap** piece of tin you tried to pass off as an expensive promise ring.

7. Woman defending her husband to her children: Yes, Dad is very **thrifty**, but he only wants what is best for you.
   A woman complaining about her husband to a friend: I swear my husband is so **tight** he told me I have to start reusing my Kleenex.

8. Woman talking to a guest: Melinda, you are so **slender** you can eat as many snickerdoodles as you want.
   Girls talking about a boy: Skip is so **skinny** he looks sick.

9. Newspaper music columnist: The very **cultured** Carlos Olivetti refuses to listen to any music except opera.
   Friends gossiping: Suzette is so **snooty** that she won't buy any of her clothes at Wal-Mart.

10. Singles ad: Ralph, a **mature** and distinguished looking man, is seeking a cute young woman to share hot fudge brownie sundaes, play dominoes and do laundry.
    Son to father: Pops, you are too **old** to understand that I need to play Star Craft much more than I need to wash the dishes.

11. Secretary to boss before an important meeting: I hate to mention it, but maybe you should change your tie. It must have gotten **soiled** at lunch.
    Mother to daughter: Sarah, your room is **filthy**, and you will not leave this house until it is clean!

12. Girl talking to veterinarian: Dr. Klinkerman, my new cat is so **timid**, she hasn't come out from under the bed in four days.
    Brother persuading sister to eat a bug: Don't be so **gutless**, Molly. Bugs are full of protein.

Answer Key
A Deal You Can Refuse, page 55

1. d
2. e
3. f
4. h
5. c
6. b
7. g
8. a

Free puppy. Good appetite, extremely affectionate, nearly house broken, very vocal. Great watch dog potential.

Answer Key
Jailbird, page 56

Dear Judge Winkner:

I'm writing to inform you that you have made a dreadful mistake by incarcerating my dear Tim. If you remember, you just sent a young and innocent Tim Weber to jail for five entire years because of a misunderstanding involving a knitting shop. Tim's heart is always in the right place, but sometimes the outside world does not recognize this about him.

You see, Your Honor, the poor boy had no money to buy his mother a birthday present because he recently lost his job because of his tendency to oversleep. (The lad has an inherited sleeping disorder.) He wanted to knit me an afghan as a gift, so I could stay warm all winter in my drafty house. This is why he needed to get his hands on some knitting equipment. Tim put his life on the line not for his own gain, but for the warmth of his mother.

I knew if you understood the reason behind Tim's misdeed and learned of Tim's caring and selfless disposition, you would recognize that you judged him too harshly. Obviously, Tim does not deserve to be put in jail at all, but I suppose you could give him some community service or maybe help him to get a new job.

Thank you in advance for releasing my son from jail.
Sincerely,
Florence Weber

Answer Key
I Love L.A., p. 57

Dear Twigs:

I hope you're having a great time in L.A. because we are all having a great time here. On Friday night, Carrie, Jen, Andy, Degan and I went to that new restaurant that opened where Babs' Bagels used to be. It is now called My Uncle Vinnie's Vittles. I ordered the lasagna, like I always do, and it was the best lasagna I ever had. Then after dinner, this really cheesy singer sat on a stool and sang ancient love songs. He even told corny jokes in between his songs, but since it was dark in there and no one could see us, we laughed and clapped for him. Afterward we drove down by the lake and met up with Jerry, Trish, Joshua and Tweet. It was really a warm night, so we sat on the grass and joked around for a while. We all miss you a lot and wish you were here to hang out with us.
Love,
Me

Answer Key
Snake Spit, p. 58

Dear Willy:

I've had it. You need to stop driving me — and the snakes — crazy every day during lunch. If you don't you're not going to have any customers or employees left.

First of all, put away the whip! When you snap it at the snakes, they go nuts. They lunge at me with their fangs out and wrap themselves around my arms until I'm too numb to reach into the bag for their Dinky Winky Snake Pellets. Pretty soon they're starving and I'm hysterical because I've got hungry snakes wrapped around my arms. I start hyperventilating and thrashing around, trying to get the snakes to let go. Customers freak out and run out of here.

You are insensitive and rude in your conduct. Either you stop, or I'm going to take a job as a cook over at the Burger Barn.

Unhappily yours,

Felix

Answer Key
Ms. Silvershine, p. 59

Ms. Emma Silvershine
1212 Goldtone Drive
Big Bucks, England

Dear Ms. Silvershine:

First of all, I would again like to thank you for your generosity. The new gourmet chef you have provided is a huge hit with counselors and campers alike. We all agree that filet mignon is much better than mystery meat deluxe.

As you know, Ms. Silvershine, all of us at Camp Runamuck think the world of you. You are not only generous but also thoughtful, kind and friendly. Because of your high standards and morals, I think you must know that your dear Kelsey is not always following your fine example. While we do appreciate Kelsey's feistiness and spunk in some situations, at other times those same traits cause quite a bit of trouble. Together, Ms. Silvershine, I think that you and a Camp Runamuck staff member need to work together to help Kelsey to funnel her energy and creativity towards good, rather than organizing underwear raids, hiding cockroaches in the head counselor's bed and putting invisible super glue around the edge of the boy's outhouse seat.

We would like to set up a time for you to come in and talk with us about Kelsey. We hope that you will work with use to help her on the road to becoming a more positive role model.

Sincerely,

Charlie Thompson, Camp Counselor

Answer Key
Get Coordinated, p. 64

1. cake and ice cream
2. Romeo and Juliet
3. green eggs and ham
4. liver and onions
5. lost and found
6. nip and tuck
7. Jack and Jill
8. black and blue
9. Shake 'n' Bake
10. rock and roll
11. hit and run
12. sticks and stones
13. lions and tigers and bears, oh my!
14. give and take
15. rise and shine
16. Ben and Jerry's
17. Mutt and Jeff
18. sweet and sour
19. sick and tired
20. song and dance

Answer Key
And You're Breathless, page 65

I hate the first second or two after I put money in a pop machine when I'm waiting for the pop to drop. I hate waiting for french fries to thaw in the microwave, for the dentist to come back to the chair with the drill, for the VCR to rewind and for commercials to end. I hate waiting for the alarm clock to go off, for Saturday, for my luggage at the airport and for my name to be called in gym class. I hate waiting for the cat to come home after her evening stroll, for the light to turn green, for my hair to grow out after a bad haircut, for spring to come, for the six o'clock news to end, for copies on the photocopy machine and for Christmas. I hate waiting for a clerk in a department store to help me find socks, for my sister to come out of the bathroom, for my other sister to get off the phone, for my brother to give me a turn on the computer, for my dad to finish reading the newspaper so he can give me a ride to my friend's house and for my mom to finish whatever she's doing so she can take me to the mall.

Answer Key
A Series of *Ands*, page 66

1. Jed, Millie, Aaron, Hong and Shawna are all expert spies.
2. I don't want to go to summer camp because I'm allergic to grass, hot marshmallows, frogs, black-roasted wieners and team sports.
3. If you teach me how to develop photographs, I'll trade you my walkie-talkies, my two goldfish, my old stereo, my blue jacket and my little brother.
4. To write poetry, you must be sensitive, clever, wise, mysterious and brave.
5. I love cake, meat, apples, Saturday and Beatrice.
6. I hate carrots, Mondays, snakes, algebra and exercise.
7. Someday I hope I can visit Belize, learn to belly dance, get the courage to try raw clams and sleep all day on a Monday.

Answer Key
Details, Details, page 67

1. It's Wednesday afternoon, and it's time to bathe the baboon.
2. Larry ran out of the room carrying the smoking VCR, and Zeb got the fire extinguisher.
3. I want to be rich, and I want to be gorgeous.
4. OK
5. I saved money for years to buy a trampoline, and now that I have one I'm too depressed to bounce.
6. OK

Answer Key
The Exclusive *Or*, page 68

1. Smile when you ask Ms. Keetz for a Kleenex, or she will be furious.
2. OK
3. OK
4. Did you hear what I said, or do you need to have your hearing checked?
5. OK
6. Do all of you have money, or should we slip around to the back?

You must talk to each other respectfully, or you'll sit in the chairs and stare at each other with no talking allowed.

All of you must agree on a TV program to watch, or I will choose it.

No biting, screaming, hitting or yelling is allowed.

You can only bounce and jump on the ugly brown couch or on the ratty old mattress in the basement.

You must turn down the volume on the television when I start to yell, or I'll hide the remote.

Answer Key
But Put in the Comma, page 69

1. Keep your eyes open, but close your mouth.
2. OK
3. OK
4. I'm going to New Jersey, but I'm going alone.
5. OK
6. I told her about Eddie, but she wouldn't believe me.
7. I will go to the play with you, but first I have to floss.
8. Taming a cobra is a chore, but it's not as dangerous as substitute teaching.
9. He seemed dead, but we noticed his hands were still warm.
10. OK
11. OK
12. Evelyn called me a zucchini-face once, but that was before I kissed her.

Never wear plaid pants to the circus, but do put a clown nose on.

You can dress your dolls in braces, but never dress your braces in dolls.

Try wearing a skirt when you ride your bike, but don't forget to wear shorts underneath.

Answer Key
For the Love of Commas, page 70

1. OK
2. I'm cancelling your debt, for our friendship means more to me than a measly million dollars.
3. OK
4. OK
5. OK
6. Goldilocks flopped into the little bear's bed, for she had travelled far and was exhausted.
7. Take your nose drops, for it is sure to rain and turn cold.
8. The chef broke down and cried, for he had lost his silver filling in the noodles.
9. OK
10. Take care of your tonsils, for they are your friends.

Never clean your room before your parents tell you to, for they will expect more out of you.

Never fall asleep first at a slumber party, for cruel shaving cream pranks will be performed on you.

Never order chow mein from China Dragon, for they make it with eel skin.

Answer Key
Yet and Nor — Say No More, page 71

1. I don't like pigeons, nor do I care to eat them.
2. OK

3. OK
4. I want to believe in Santa Claus, yet here are all these uneaten cookies.
5. I don't believe in you and your ideas, nor do I believe in this tonic.
6. OK
7. Jane hasn't called, nor has she written in over ten years.
8. OK
9. OK
10. OK
11. I knew you liked rubber cement, yet I didn't think you would eat it.
12. OK

It is a good idea to insist that your children eat vegetables, yet it is probably a waste of time to give them Brussel sprouts.
Children usually tell their parents the truth, yet they often leave out important details.
Never give a neurotic dachshund a squeaky toy, nor let your children try to dress him up in baby clothes.

Answer Key
Either/Or . . . Neither/Nor, page 72

1. either/or
2. neither/nor
3. either/or
4. either/or
5. neither/nor
6. neither/nor
7. either/or
8. neither/nor
9. either/or
10. neither/nor
11. either/or
12. neither/nor

The Ding-A-Ling Brothers Circus promised an evening of laughter and spectacular family entertainment. Unfortunately, my family **neither** laughed **nor** felt entertained during the two hour show. Instead we **either** yawned **or** nodded off every now and then. Even the performers seemed bored. The clowns strolled into the arena and **either** did only a few half-hearted gags **or** just stood there doing nothing at all. The elephants **neither** followed instructions **nor** performed any tricks at all. The dogs ran around playing with a frisbee instead of jumping through hoops. It was not a night to remember.

Answer Key

		Use Them or Lose Them, page 73
1. and/but	8. but (or for)	
2. and	9. nor	
3. or	10. for	
4. for	11. or	
5. yet (or but)	12. nor	
6. but	13. for	
7. and	14. or	

I hate it when my sister eats a peanut butter and jelly sandwich and then breathes on me, but I hate it even more when she paws through a can of nuts to get all the cashews.

Answer Key
Make Your Own, page 74

1. I found my accordion in the Dumpster, but I don't know who put it there.
2. My grandma said she'd get me a hamster or a gerbil for my birthday, but not both.
3. Eat a morsel of spinach or you won't be going to the Sizzlin' Squash concert tonight.
4. Neither double-cocoa cheese cake nor peachy-pumpkin pecan tarts will tempt me from my new diet.
5. The vampire frightened the reindeer, but they got out of his way.
6. Herschel was very happy as a ghost, yet he was lonely for Melinda, his true love, who was still roaming the earth.
7. The detective searched every apartment on the east side of Chicago, but he couldn't find the hostage.
8. Mr. Ronowicz knew Geraldine could give him the correct answer, but she never raised her hand or volunteered to talk in class.
9. I'd like to write a song about an inchworm, but what would I say?
10. Dante longed to play the keyboard or the trombone in a band, but he never wanted to practice.

Answer Key
Write On, page 75

Pop artist Coolie Julie Smite was seen wandering the halls of Wishweewurowtuvhere High School last Thursday afternoon. Coolie Julie is famed for her songs "Smells Like Teen Sweat" and "Writin' On the Bathroom Walls," **but** the song that shot her to the top of the billboard charts was her ballad, "Don't Let Leonardo Die On the Titanic."

Before she visited, neither the staff **nor** the students of WHS realized that Coolie Julie is the cousin of Principal Smith Smite. "Coolie Julie is so cool that it's hard to believe she is related to Principal Smite, **yet** they do have the same last name," commented one student.

Coolie Julie is in town for the Smite family reunion that is taking place on Saturday in the downtown park. Only family members are invited, **and** they will have to show identification to be admitted into the party.

For those of you wanting to catch a glimpse of Coolie Julie, you can do so either from a distance on Saturday at the park **or** on Friday at 2:00 PM at the high school, where she will be performing. If you do decide to go to the concert, our advice is to take earplugs, **for** her music is very loud.

Answer Key
Subordinating Conjunctions, page 76

Cheri loves aardvarks, although she has never owned one.
Mikey eats mangoes, although he prefers enchiladas.
Evelyn loves winter, although she's afraid of the snow.
(Each of the sentences could also begin with the subordinating conjunction "although.")

Answer Key
Subordinating Combos, page 77

1. **Whenever** I see an aquarium, I want to jump into it and blow bubbles against the glass.
2. Edwina keeps showing up at the circus **because** she hopes the Great Valentino will throw her a kiss from the high wire.
3. Dawn loves company, **although** she prefers that her guests sleep in the yard.
4. **Since** Pat learned to cook last summer, no one feels safe.

5. **Because** Gabe hates meatloaf, he stuffed his sandwich into Felicia's French horn.
6. **Until** he got the measles, Spot was a decent-looking dog.
7. **If** you give me the keys to your car, I won't tell how you rigged the fog machine to belch.

Answer Key
The Making of a Dependent Clause, page 78

1. Although Amy buttered the toast, she wouldn't eat it.
2. Since Mavis lost her sandals, she had to wear sneakers.
3. Until Albert believes in himself, he'll never be able to ski the steepest peak in the resort.
4. Whenever people sneeze in crowded elevators, Shelly pushes the emergency button so she can get off immediately.
5. Although nobody believed Wilbur could have won, there was his name on the trophy.
6. Jody placed the custard pie in the box and mailed it, although she knew it would never arrive in one piece.
7. It became obvious that Mark was hallucinating when he said he had slammed his locker shut on a "mid-sized purple frog with crooked teeth and a heavy French accent."
8. Margot ate all the carbohydrates in the house whenever she had to study for a big test.

Answer Key
Subordinatium Gladiloli, page 79

You know, no one respects a fern. **If** I had been propagated as an orchid, I might get a little more respect. I might have moved to a penthouse on Park Avenue, instead of being plopped down on a cold, hard, white table in the cafeteria of Lancelot Junior High. The students here give me about as much respect as they give the head cook, Frieda, which isn't much. They hate her.

Although the students don't respect Frieda or me, they respect Frances, the lunchroom monitor. She won't let students go outside **until** they have eaten all of their spinach, which is another leafy plant that gets no respect. **When** Frances isn't looking, students sometimes shove their hot, slimy spinach into my soil. The spinach burns my roots and smells putrid. Frankly, I hate spinach too.

My life is miserable. I hate the buzzing glare of fluorescent lights and the smell of Frieda's lemony ammonia cleaner. Most of all, I hate smelling the prune bars Frieda whips up every Friday morning **after** she comes to work.

Answer Key
The Case of the Pronoun Prank, page 84

(A total of 19 pronouns)

Brian walked into the room with no intention of doing any mischief until **he** saw **his** grandmother's false teeth in a glass on the lamp stand next to **her** bed. **He** approached the false teeth with a smile on **his** face. What a find! **He** knew exactly what **he** would do. **He** sneaked down to the kitchen and opened the refrigerator. **He** saw trays full of cheese snacks, and **he** knew who **they** were for — **his** mother's bridge club friends who came over every Thursday night. Brian (or **he**) slipped the teeth out of **his** pocket and stuffed **them** inside the bacon-onion dip. Then **he** closed the door and went upstairs. That night, from far below in the dining room, **he** heard his mother's guests. **Their** screams drifted up to **him** in sharp, pleasant waves.

Answer Key
Getting Personal, page 85

1. When I turned on the lie detector, **it** told me **it** had a headache. Honest!

2. If the doctor ever shows up, ask **her** (**him**) if **she** (**he**) will deliver the baby.
3. "I can't believe you ate 39 kumquats," said Tom to **his** brother.
4. Gertrude threw the banana cream pie at the judge, but **she** later apologized.
5. Alvin asked Tim to loan **him** **his** skateboard, but Tim said, "Buy your own!"

Main points to make in speech:

We have a great team, and **we** deserve to be here.
We were a success in Loose Tooth, and know **we** can be a success anywhere.
If **we** can play so successfully wearing restricting mittens, imagine what **we** can do with **our** bare hands!
Join **me** in this cheer: Ring, ring, lift and toss — **We'll** show the other team who's the boss!

Answer Key
"Self" Pronouns, page 86

1. themselves
2. himself
3. yourselves
4. herself
5. herself
6. yourself
7. myself
8. itself
9. oneself
10. ourselves

Dear Mrs. Ajax:
    You seem to be a woman who prides **herself** on producing a quality chocolate. I'm here to commend you on a job well done. In fact, I take it upon **myself** to help you make your chocolate even better; I would like to be your chocolate taster.
    Don't feel that you have to pay me for my services. My reward is in knowing that your quality chocolates are gracing the earth's surface (or my stomach). In fact, I swear to test every little piece of chocolate that comes my way. Your profits may go down, but quality will remain superior, I assure you. A man should consider **himself** lucky to get even one precious piece of Ajax chocolate.
    Your chocolates will be in great demand thanks to me and my mighty tastebuds. Think about it.
Impatiently salivating,
Tootsie Jones

Answer Key
Always Single, page 87

1. is
2. has
3. is
4. wants
5. has
6. likes
7. winks
8. is
9. wants
10. likes

Answer Key
Everyone's Favorite, page 88

1. has
2. does
3. loves
4. listens
5. is
6. happens
7. goes
8. wants
9. loves
10. gags

1. As I look around the gorgeous old room, I wonder if **anyone** else is as confused as I am?
2. The singing is beautiful, but I can't understand any of the words. Does **anyone** else?
3. **Everything** is so precise and artistic. What are they singing about?
4. **Somebody** help me, I'm so bored!
5. Oh, I get it! You are supposed to read the program to understand the story and then watch **every-one** on stage to understand the emotion and ideas. **Nobody** told me that!

Answer Key
Pronouns of Your Own, page 89

1. Everyone but me wants to see the depressing movie about the sinking ship.
2. Neither of the elves thinks Santa pays his employees well enough.
3. One of the oranges mysteriously rolls down the hallway by itself whenever marmalade is mentioned.
4. Nobody with a grain of sense goes to the haunted house on Raven Lane at night.
5. Everything in the fish tank has a curious green tint to it.
6. "Either of the boys will do," said the wicked witch with a mean grin and an oven mitt on her hand.
7. Each of the eggplants is beautiful in its own purpley way.
8. Something in the cellar smells like my Great Aunt Tilly's kitchen.
9. Each of the incidents can be explained by the existence of an alien mother ship hidden in the clouds.
10. Neither of the cows thinks beef jerky jokes are funny.

Answer Key
Find Them and Fix Them, page 90

line #1:   "Everyone **believes** . . ."
line #2:   "Each of her brothers **is** . . ."
line #3:   "everybody **was** having . . .", "someone **was** learning . . ."
line #5:   "No one could **believe** it."
line #6:   "No one **was** . . ."
line #8:   "Everybody **was** . . ."
line #13:   "Neither of the clerks **was** . . ."
line #14:   "One of the broccoli bunches **was** . . ."
line #21:   "when no one **was** . . ."
line #25:   "Neither of the managers **was** . . ."
line #28:   "Everyone else **believes** . . ."

Answer Key
Possessive Pronouns, page 91

We never get to fly on **our** vacations. We always have to drive. **My** parents say it is because they want to save **their** money for other things, rather than spending it all on air fare. But the "other things" they spend it on are pretty stupid — like when we drove 700 miles to go to a Star Trek convention. I begged and begged **my** mom not to wear **her** fake Mr. Spock ears, but she did it anyway. "They're **mine** and I'll do what I want with them," she explained in Klingon. I had to ask **my** sister for **her** Klingon dictionary just so I could translate. And of course I always get carsick on these trips. I just can't handle the way **my** dad drives. It's almost like he's having spasms in **his** foot or something, the way he presses on the gas and then presses on the brake and then the gas again. I always hope that he'll press more on the gas than the brake so we can get back to **our** house sooner.

Answer Key
Non-Sexist Pronouns, page 92

1. All the students kept their cool during the food fight.
2. No one did any homework over the weekend, so everyone failed.
3. People who love their dogs should avoid large, vicious cats.
4. Somebody left a pair of dirty socks on the bus.
5. Everybody filled up at the taco bar.

Answer Key
It's All Relative, page 93

1. Nobody came to the beach party **that** was held in Mary's dad's garage.
2. I like mystery stories **that** don't have butlers, knives or English castles looming in the fog.
3. My teacher was a tall woman **who** wore red hats and plastic shoes when she wasn't in school.
4. My neighbor once owned a cocker spaniel **whose** pups bit into their mother's ears and hung on like wood ticks.
5. Joey has a nickname **that** he hates.

Answer Key
Pronouns Out of Place, page 94

1. The trainer turned to the crowd and said, "We need someone who is absolutely odorless to jump into the tank with Boris the shark."
2. Julio bought cotton candy that was way too sweet from a girl at the fair.
3. I'd like to hire someone who doesn't smoke to feed and train our horse.
4. Never trust a lady who walks everywhere in high heels with a dog.
5. At the race track, which was oval shaped and 300 yards wide, I saw a horse.
6. I met two men who wore chrome-plated sunglasses and carried smoked fish.

Answer Key
Writing With Relatives, page 95

1. This is a new flotation device **that** instantly inflates to the size of a St. Bernard and dog-paddles you to safety.
2. We are looking for a new photographer's assistant **who** must be able to distract children for at least 30 seconds, using distorted facial expressions.
3. Our circus needs a new act, **which** must have pizazz, pizoom and free balloons.

4. Across the vast distance of the Grand Canyon hung a massive black web, **which** everyone knew was the work of Spiderman.
5. The police are searching for a distraught woman **whose** chimpanzee apparently stole the family car and left for St. Louis.

Answer Key
All Alone in the World, page 100

1. Wow! Three large pizzas, and no one is home but me.
2. Whoa! I can't write as fast as you think.
3. Yikes! It's hotter in here than the inside of a jalapeno pepper.
4. I'm sure, well, actually I'm pretty sure I did it right.
5. Halt! This is your principal speaking.
6. Say — would you like to win a trip to Disneyland?
7. Great Scott! Your teeth have all turned yellow.

Hank swaggered across the crowded gym to the tall, stunning brunette standing by the punch bowl. "**Wow**! You look great!" exclaimed Hank, when he realized the woman was none other than Nora Finklestein.

"**Well**, you sound a little surprised about that," accused Nora.

"You did have a rather large acne problem back in school. Not to mention the bad perm you always had and the hideous clothes you used to wear," Hank explained.

"Obviously, people can change." Nora smiled, as she stared right at Hank's large belly and shiny bald head.

Hank had no idea she had insulted him. "**Hey**, baby," he said. "How about you and I split this lame party and go for a ride?" He put his arm around her.

Nora grabbed a bowl of whipped cream from the sundae bar, dumped it on Hank's bald head and topped him with a maraschino cherry. "This is for all the horrible and mean things you, Hank the handsome high school hunk, did to us so-called nerds," she said. Then the whole gym erupted in cheers.

Answer Key
Hey! This Is Serious, page 101

Me:	Let's go to a movie, Kelly.
Kelly:	Great! I'd love to! It will be such fun!
Me:	I'd like to see "Halloween, Part 23."
Kelly:	Ooh! I'm sure it would be too scary!
Me:	How about "Love in the Springtime?"
Kelly:	Yes! I love love stories. And we'll get popcorn. I love popcorn!
Me:	Okay. But I'll probably just get Milk Duds.
Kelly:	Yes! I love Milk Duds, too! And Raisinettes! Or anything chocolate!
Me:	Okay, shall we ask Alex to come along?
Kelly:	Oh yes! Alex is so much fun! I just love her! And let's ask Andrea and Marcia, too!
Me:	Well, okay, I guess.
Kelly:	Great! I can't wait! I'll go call the others!

Answer Key
Holy Bat Wings!, page 102

1. Gooey goulash! This must have been in the refrigerator for four and a half months!
2. Holy guacamole! This dip is hot!
3. Great bananas! We had better split!

4. Galloping grapes! We get to visit a vineyard!
5. Wacky wontons! We should have made reservations!
6. Leapin' lasagna! This pasta is fabulous.
7. Suffering salsa! I never knew tamales were this hard to make.
8. Lucky latte! There's a silver dollar in my coffee!
9. Hoppin' hamburgers! My meat is so rare it's still mooing!
10. Blazing bricks! I think there's a fire in the chimney.

Answer Key
Adverbs? How?, page 106

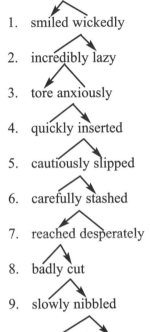

1. smiled wickedly

2. incredibly lazy

3. tore anxiously

4. quickly inserted

5. cautiously slipped

6. carefully stashed

7. reached desperately

8. badly cut

9. slowly nibbled

10. completely ignores

Elizabeth bravely faced the dangerous enemy.
Melanie cautiously examined her haircut and bawled.
A tornado abruptly descended upon the town and tore it apart.

Answer Key
Adverbs? Where?, page 107

1. forward
2. around
3. behind
4. back

First, go **out** of your classroom and turn **right**. Walk **forward** to the staircase by locker bay number seven. Then walk down the up ramp to the gym. When you get to the bottom of the ramp, turn left and take 10 giant steps **backward**. Tiptoe into the boys locker room. Walk **up** to the showers and look behind the third moldy shower curtain from the right. There you will find your restroom pass.

Answer Key
The Case of the Adverb Clue, page 108

1. nowhere
2. anywhere
3. everywhere
4. somewhere
5. elsewhere

When Mr. Rhodes called in sick on the day of the science field trip, mousy Miss Wolfenbarger was the substitute. After a wild and crazy bus drive to Lake Minirumpus, students got off the bus and ran **everywhere**. Some students hid under the bridge; others climbed a tree; some jumped in the lake; and a few were **nowhere** to be found. Miss Wolfenbarger buried her head in her trembling hands and prayed, "Please take me away! I would rather be **anywhere** but here at Lake Minirumpus."

She tried to round up the students and take them back to school, where they would be someone else's problem. She searched **everywhere** and found many of them, but she couldn't find six of the biggest troublemakers. Finally, she told the bus driver to leave. "I don't care if those snotty kids have to spend the night here," she shrieked.

When they returned to the school, Miss Wolfenbarger jumped in her car and sped out of the parking lot as fast as she could. She decided right then and there to get a new job that would be **nowhere** near kids or schools.

Answer Key
Adverbs? When?, page 109

1. someday
2. never
3. before
4. later
5. Eventually
6. Suddenly

Before I went to my stepmother's nephew's wedding, I thought that going to a wedding might be fun. After the seven bridesmaids took 30 minutes to come down the aisle, I changed my mind. However, I sat still because Dad promised that immediately after the wedding, we would go back to our hotel and swim in the pool.

Answer Key
Adverbs? To What Extent?, page 110

1. Marty's gym locker has a rather interesting smell.
2. I am somewhat fond of Jenny's older brother Alfonse.
3. My report card is largely satisfactory.
4. Yes, Timmy can be quite difficult sometimes, but I still won't pay you double for babysitting him.
5. English is clearly my best subject.

Answer Key
Adverbs . . . Not Just for Verbs Anymore, page 111

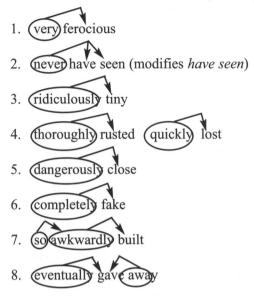

1. (very) ferocious

2. (never) have seen (modifies *have seen*)

3. (ridiculously) tiny

4. (thoroughly) rusted (quickly) lost

5. (dangerously) close

6. (completely) fake

7. (so) (awkwardly) built

8. (eventually) gave (away)

Elaine Hidalgo stupidly agreed to let Jason Bickerman buckle her into The Bullet. He sometimes worked at the old carnival and didn't know everything, like how the oddly rusted metal lap bars could get stuck shut. Because he had a sickeningly sweet crush on Elaine, Jason made sure he closed her lap belt extremely hard so she wouldn't fall out.

Answer Key
Lights! Action! Adverbs!, page 112

1. *Always In Your Locker* — An **incredibly** important homework assignment is never found, despite **desperate** rummaging, because it is **hopelessly** lost in the locker zone.
2. *Tentative Showering* — Chris Carter stars as a boy who fights **non-stop** to end the **dreadfully** awful act of **communal** showering at his junior high school.
3. *Sappy Love Letters* — Humor abounds as an **amazingly sappy** love note gets **wrongly** passed from one student to another.
4. *Never On the Bus* — A **frighteningly** stuffy bus driver's attempts to create silent and well-behaved students on her bus backfires **horribly**.

Answer Key
Tagging Along, page 113

1. flatly
2. fittingly
3. quizzically
4. dramatically
5. slowly
6. sheepishly
7. haltingly
8. hollowly
9. aimlessly
10. speedily

"Where's my scarf and hat?" Frosty the Snowman said coldly.

"Turn on the Christmas tree," Father said brightly.

"I'll huff and puff and blow your house down," said the wolf breathlessly.

"Just tell me how many scoops of ice cream you want," the Baskin-Robbins clerk said icily.

"This building will be the biggest in the city," said the architect constructively.

Answer Key
Adverb Overflow, page 114

Beauty and the Beast is the story of an intelligent, dreamy-headed girl named Belle, who lives in a small village with her aging father, who is a somewhat fumbling inventor. He spends all day creating strange machines that often don't work.

One day he decides to travel to the fair to demonstrate his latest invention, but he gets lost on the way. He walks to the creepy castle of the Beast, who traps the old man in a nasty prison. Belle comes looking for her father and exchanges herself for her father, who is ill. The Beast treats her badly at first, but he eventually falls deeply in love with her.

Meanwhile, she learns of the incredible legend surrounding the lonely beast. He must be loved truly and simply by someone in order for the awful spell of ugliness to be broken. Belle eventually learns to love him, but not before the Beast's castle is stormed and the jealous character Gaston viciously stabs the beast, fatally wounding him. The Beast shoves Gaston to his death, then gasps his last long breath and dies. Belle kisses him, and the Beast comes to life and is transformed into a handsome prince. Belle and the Prince live happily ever after.

Answer Key
Party Time, page 115

I knew this would be a **completely** awful party from the moment I walked in the door and the heavy scent of warmed buttermilk hit my nostrils. All of my friends stood **stupidly** near the exits, staring **numbly** into space while Harry Gainey danced **foolishly** to the orchestra music. When Harry started to plead **urgently** for someone to turn up the bass, the chaperones called his parents. I was **absolutely** sure it was time to leave and went with some friends to the Taco Bell across the street for some **unbelievably** cheap burritos. I would **never** go to anther party like that one.